WORDPLAYS 2

WORDPLAYS 2

© 1982 Copyright by Performing Arts Journal Publications

Chucky's Hunch: © 1981, 1982 Copyright by Rochelle Owens
A Thought in Three Parts: © 1975, 1982 Copyright by Wallace Shawn
Dark Ride: © 1981, 1982 Copyright by Len Jenkin
The Brides: © 1980, 1982 Copyright by Harry Kondoleon
All Night Long: © 1979, 1982 Copyright by John O'Keefe

First Edition
All rights reserved
No part of this publication may be reproduced or transmitted in any form or by any means, electronic or mechanical, including photocopy, recording, or any information storage or retrieval system now known or to be invented, without permission in writing from the publishers, except by a reviewer who wishes to quote brief passages in connection with a review written for inclusion in a magazine, newspaper, or broadcast.

Library of Congress Cataloging in Publication Data
Wordplays 2
Library of Congress Catalog Card No.: 82-62155
ISBN: 0-933826-42-7
ISBN: 0-933826-43-5 (paper)

All rights reserved under the International and Pan-American Copyright Conventions. For information, write to Performing Arts Journal Publications, 325 Spring Street, Room 318, New York, N.Y. 10013.

For production rights, refer to individual plays. Professionals and amateurs are warned that the plays appearing herein are fully protected under the Copyright Laws of the United States and all other countries of the Copyright Union. All rights including professional, amateur, motion picture, recitation, lecturing, public readings, radio and television broadcasting, and the rights of translation into foreign languages, are strictly reserved.

Design: Gautam Dasgupta
Printed in the United States of America

PAJ Playscripts/General Editors:
Bonnie Marranca and Gautam Dasgupta

Publication of this book has been made possible in part by a grant from the National Endowment for the Arts, Washington, D.C., a federal agency, and public funds received from the New York State Council on the Arts.

WORDPLAYS 2

an anthology of New American Drama

Performing Arts Journal Publications
New York City

THE WORDPLAYS SERIES

We published the first edition of *Wordplays: New American Drama* in 1980, and the book's reception, both in the theatre and in places where theatre is taught, was so positive that we decided to expand the concept into a series. So this volume, *Wordplays 2,* continues that series.

Wordplays is about new approaches to writing for the theatre by American playwrights. We choose plays that we think audiences should know about, hoping that this will give the plays a longer life in the theatre through productions. Sometimes we include writers who have never been published before, others who are not known throughout the country but we feel they should be, and we always want to publish writers who already have a history in the theatre.

For us, the most important thing is that the writing go beyond the cliché into something more provocative, even more difficult at times, to bring us closer to the kind of characters, the feeling of communication, of time, and of space, and the processes of thinking that outline the contemporary experience of living. Our hope is that this ongoing *Wordplays* Series embraces the panorama of styles and temperaments reflected in contemporary American plays.

The Publishers

PAJ PLAYSCRIPT SERIES

General Editors: Bonnie Marranca and Gautam Dasgupta

OTHER TITLES IN THE SERIES:

THEATRE OF THE RIDICULOUS/Kenneth Bernard, Charles Ludlam, Ronald Tavel

ANIMATIONS: A TRILOGY FOR MABOU MINES/Lee Breuer

THE RED ROBINS/Kenneth Koch

THE WOMEN'S PROJECT/Penelope Gilliatt, Lavonne Mueller, Rose Leiman Goldemberg, Joyce Aaron-Luna Tarlo, Kathleen Collins, Joan Schenkar, Phyllis Purscell

WORDPLAYS: NEW AMERICAN DRAMA/Maria Irene Fornes, Ronald Tavel, Jean-Claude van Itallie, Richard Nelson, William Hauptman, John Wellman

BEELZEBUB SONATA/Stanislaw I. Witkiewicz

DIVISION STREET AND OTHER PLAYS/Steve Tesich

TABLE SETTINGS/James Lapine

THE PRESIDENT AND EVE OF RETIREMENT/Thomas Bernhard

TWELVE DREAMS/James Lapine

SICILIAN COMEDIES/Luigi Pirandello

THE ENTHUSIASTS/Robert Musil

Contents

Chucky's Hunch/Rochelle Owens — 9

A Thought in Three Parts/Wallace Shawn — 29

Dark Ride/Len Jenkin — 59

The Brides/Harry Kondoleon — 97

All Night Long/John O'Keefe — 117

Playwrights' Biographies — 166

KEVIN O'CONNOR IN "CHUCKY'S HUNCH"

Chucky's Hunch

Rochelle Owens

Chucky's Hunch was produced by Theatre for the New City (Crystal Field and George Bartenieff, artistic directors) in New York City on March 22, 1981, with the following cast:

CHUCKY..*Kevin O'Connor*

Director: Elinor Renfield
Sets: Abe Lubelski
Costumes: Carla Kramer
Lighting: Peter Kaczorowski
Sound: Paul Garrity

Chucky's Hunch reopened at the Harold Clurman Theatre in New York City on February 16, 1982.

© 1981, 1982 Copyright by Rochelle Owens.
CAUTION: No performances or readings of this work may be given without the express authorization of the author. For production rights, contact: Rochelle Owens, 606 West 116th. Street, New York, N.Y. 10027.

CHARACTER: CHUCKY

A man with graying hair wearing a turtleneck sweater and a worn shapeless tweed jacket. He is a failed artist of about fifty years old. He is sitting on a worn upholstered chair, a foot-stool is near. There is a table next to him; on it are a few random carpenter's tools, a decanter of water, and a wooden bird-feeder construction.

A note concerning direction.

A monologue created out of a series of never-answered letters to Chucky's ex-wife Elly who at times he calls by other names. Chucky is never in the act of writing the letters. The direction should focus on the humorous as well as the darker aspects of the inner and outer world of Chucky. His voice reveals anger, arrogance, contempt, cynicism, envy, glee, mockery, self-pity, spite and torment.

The play may be presented with a simplified interior setting, and a minimum of props. The director can decide whether or not to actually present Chucky's mother or to have a voice on tape. The musical transitions may be substituted.

CHUCKY:
Okay, so you and I cut through some of those lies over twenty years ago. Beginning in 1956. That's cool. My message to you now is: Elly, who are YOU talking to? Dear Della, remember the Christmas when we hitchhiked across the country together? It was in 1958. Dig? And the young trucker asked

us if we lived like that—picking up rides across the U.S.A. The joker was amazed, wiped out by our pre-hippy lifestyle. But he didn't know a thing about us because, and I must repeat, because we never told him our names! He who knows my name has power over me! Shit—I never wrote my name big enough for you—you refugee from Brooklyn. Ethnic! Oh, I beg your pardon, I promised myself this is going to be a polite communication. I just wanted to congratulate you for winning all that dough in the lottery, Elly. Hey, you never answered any of my other letters. What's the matter—Whatsis Face wouldn't let you? You know what I did today?—I fed Freddy and the puppies. Yup. Freddy is my four-year-old husky. What a beautiful dog. He and the puppies are in the room next to Ma's room. Yup, here we are, the two of us, my eighty-five-year-old Ma and I, in her dilapidated dream house. What a stink-pit. You and Whatsis Face ought to come out and take a look. Hey, I'll even build a fire for you. Poor old Ma—little did she know that her blue-eyed boy would come to such a bad end. The old woman just lies in bed fifteen hours a day. I can't blame her—what the fuck is there to get up for? Last night I got smashed and I was stalking through the old house with a hammer in my hand. The furnace was on the blink and I was trying to fix it but I also knew that old Ma was kinda scared of me. We'd had a fight. She gets mad because she has to help support me on her Social Security checks. She says I'm just like George. You remember who he was—my father! Well, you know I never knew my father. He was no good and old American, as Ma says, and I'm an awful lot like him and she sure stresses the word "awful." But I'm an artist, remember—an abstract expressionist that is. And you're just a housewife. I have this book that I've been working on a few years now—you and Whatsis Face ought to read it. It tells the way it is and was—it even goes into the American art world scene and I like to think that it's a metaphor for the American political scene as well. You have to be a hustler to make it big. Hey, have you heard the one about the ethnic who goes to get gas? Ah, you wouldn't get the gist of it—you just wouldn't get the gist. Speakin' of ethnics—the way these Portuguese here in town treat me when I go to their goddamned one and only bar—you'd think I was the local, I don't know what—pervert! I was talking to Marie the waitress about it the other night. Boy, I'd love to get into a knock-down drag-out fight with her. Prone position—we might really make some sense together. Hey, how's Whatsis Face? Can he hear with all the wax in his ears? That's gonna be the title of my next book: *Earwax of America's Minorities*. You know, ineluctable Della, what really grinds your jaws as well as pissing you off—is my own failings! *C'est vrai?* It's the times. The times, dearie. My own failings are enmeshed with the times! Is that problematic enough for you—you refugee from Brooklyn! You . . . But let's not get impolite, Chucky. Nope. I'm going to restrain myself. Be cool. Hey, Elly, you still like to munch on chicken legs? I remember you used to like to talk about philosophical subjects when you had a piece of chicken between your fingers. Dig? Well, again, I just wanted to congratulate you on winnng the lottery. Remember Ms. Housewife—the profit-making system never contaminated me. Sincerely, Chucky. An American Artist.

(Lights dim. Taped music of "Greensleeves" offstage.)

Dear Della-Fella,

May I call you Della-Fella? You think that's an irrelevant question, don't you? Well, don't you? You middle-class babe in the woods. Wow! Here I go again, and I wanted to get off on the right side of the sack with you. Dig? All kidding aside, I spoke to our mutal friend Ronnie some weeks ago and he said you look insane. Hey, Della-Fella, when you decided to walk out on me twenty years ago because I was too much of an artist for the likes of a bourgeois cunt like you really are—even though you conned a lot of members of the earwax generation into believing you might be an artist—did you ever dream that I'd end up here in this neck of the woods? Living with my 85-year-old mother in a rotting pre-Revolutionary house in a remote part of upstate New York? Hey, wow, I started my drinking at ten this morning before I got old Ma her breakfast. Yeah, Ma was having her bacon and eggs and Sonny-boy was taking his first snort. Then my dog Freddy took a leak on the laundry that I brought back spanking clean from the laundromat. Ma's gonna yell bloody murder when she smells her sheets. And yesterday morning I went to my new employer to ask for an advance on my salary and the mean bitch turned me down because I already owe her fifty bucks. She told me she's going to call the cops if I continue to bother her. Bother her? Shit! Well, fuck it! Tomorrow's a new day and I'm going to renovate this beautiful old church in town—I asked them if I could—incredible stained-glass windows—like the rose window at Chartres. Remember? Sometimes I start thinking of when I was seven years old sitting on my grandmother's porch in Michigan, holding a glass of cold water and a chocolate nut cookie—and then I think of what Ma always says—how did I ever get out of the mid-West alive? Anyway, back at the ranch, guffaw, guffaw! I mean I seriously am going to renovate this gothic-style church. Hey, why don't you ever call me up? I gave you my phone number. Tell Whatsis Face that he's welcome to read my novel also. Did I ever tell you that I had this beautiful parrot that could whistle and some bastard shot him? And did I ever tell you that Sally, the girl I married after you, Della-Fella, had a baby by an East Indian and the baby's rear-end was covered with black spots? Wow! I used to be able to fuck a lot. Ha! Marie, the waitress, says I'm the only middle-aged adolescent she knows. I'm going to be fifty soon, and my teeth are rotting away. Heaven help me. Your faithful friend, Chucky. P.S. Please excuse my rudeness. I got carried away. I really would like some contact and to be able to feel like a member of the human race once again. C.C.

(Lights dim. Taped music of Italian madrigals offstage. Then, lights up.)

Dear Della-Fella,

  See what you made me do? Yeah, you did it, kiddo. Anybody ever tell you about yourself—like I did?—literally uncorking that dumb little housewife's mind that's stuck somewhere between your ears? Put that in your pipe and smoke it! Dig? I'm sitting here now—after scolding the puppies for teasing Freddy—named after the famous and important Freddy Held who made it big in the New York art scene. Freddy Held, yeah. How could a boy like me and from the mid-West ever compete with the biggies from the city. Oops, there I go again digressing—Ma says that I'm the most digressing person she's ever seen—and she ought to know after all the times we've digressed each other. But you know my story, dear Elly. I could tell Whatsis Face much more easily than I could tell you how women have always lorded it over me. You are part of the problem. Forget the Freudian chicken soup—you refugee from Brooklyn! The trouble is I know whatever Chucky wants Chucky gets—I also know the real trouble is that Chucky doesn't always know what he wants. After you and I split up—when I was with my third wife, Sally, in 1961, I went into the antique business. Yeah, I knew that would make you laugh—but I had a little antique shop—and then everything started to fall apart—I mean the bottom of my life was starting to drop out—maybe I'm too nervous! Shucks, look what you got me doing—complaining about the conditions of my life. Now don't tell me to see a shrink because I tried it. It didn't work! I know, my perceptions at times are completely messed up. But not nearly as messed up and rotten as yours must be—No! No! No! I refuse to let you get worked up in defense of yourself! You really ought to care about what happens to your fellow human beings in this world which is part of the cosmos. You ought to because it is your responsibility to! My mother's legs are mapped all over with varicose veins and she's a dope addict. What difference does it make because she's 85? Are you saying that? Well, when I look in the mirror I see someone I don't recognize who gets mad at his mother for growing too old to care anymore about her legs, or even having din-din in a little restaurant. Oh, how incorrigible I yam, I yam. Yeah. But just remember I was more intelligent than you! I WAS MORE INTELLIGENT THAN YOU! Boy, I got you worked up. This time I really got a rise outta you. Listen, between the phonies of the big shitty, yeah New York is the big shitty. Heh, heh, heh. Anyway between the phonies—I repeat the phonies of the art world scene and you—it's a wonder that the magic christian ever got out alive! Remember Della-Fella, if I wanted to suck seed, yeah, suck seed—I could have—but I didn't want to. Listen dearie, drop me a line or two. I'm sure we can communicate—maybe we can even meet in a hotel room somewhere and finally fight it out. Remember the mosaic that I did over twenty years ago? The knight with his lovely lady. He was playing the lute—and she sat there next to him—with an empty smile. Your American Artist. Charles.

(*Lights dim. Taped music of jazz. Music stops. Lights up.*)

Dear Elly,

In spite of your winning the lottery ticket, you're a failure! You and I are both failures. Do you dig it? And so is Ma. You know what happened to her today? She slipped in the bathtub and fell down real hard on her ass—she accused me of pushing her! I was only trying to help her out of the goddamn tub! The phone company ought to be bombed like Con Edison was in the '60s. Actually, Con Edison was never bombed, but there was this sore loser who had a grudge and intended to bomb Con Ed. My grudge is against the phone company. Hey, what do you think of a person who makes crank calls? Do you think he's crazy? Do you think that individual has a grudge against somebody? Hey, Della-Fella, how come you never had a kid? Where have all the children gone, long time passing . . . ?

You remember in 1958 when I was interviewed by that young twerp from the Columbia School of Journalism and he suspected that I was of a rebellious nature. And he told me, "We can't afford to have defiant characters in our midst." Hey, Della, did you think that I was a defiant character? I was really too much for you, wasn't I? From the very first day that I met you when I told you about my life with my first wife, Hettie, you thought of me as the sonovabitch in your life. But at least you came close to knowing a real artist. I'm sure about certain things. In the same way that the French Impressionists knew that the emphasis on the quality of light would separate them from the meat and brown gravy of the traditionalist school. From Rembrandt. It's in my book. It's *all* in my book. I want to send you my book because you're in it too. It's about you, Della. The book's about you. Do you remember my old hernia operation? The fissure that I have on my side? It still oozes sometimes. My old hernia trouble. It sounds like a song. God what a disgusting mess I yam, I yam. But I still get horny. The other night I took a package of beef kidneys that were supposed to be for the cats, yup, we have two of them running around. I let the kidneys get at room temperature, then I wrapped them in a pair of panties and somehow managed to work myself up into a state of sexual desire—and came into the kidneys. Pretty depraved, right? Do you remember during the fifties you used to wear your dark red lipstick over your lipline, a fat round arc that glistened—you were stacked like a brick shithouse. You were my foot-stool, Elly. I just had an image of you eating with your head bent way over close to the kitchen table, without your eyeglasses you were almost blind. It took guts and patience for you to get used to the contact lenses that I bought for you. Please try to show a little gratitude. Your faithful former husband, Chucky.

(*Lights dim. Taped music of jazz. Music stops. Black-out.*)

Dear Elly,
You ole rubber hammer, you. I'm sorry for coming on strong. Forgive Chucky. It's a deal? Cool. I'll start again more politely. Dear Della. Last

night Ma began her usual lecture, that is when I remove her muzzle she starts her yapping. Boy she can sure bug a man. Anyway, she began as always, stressing the two most important qualities a civilized human being must have: A sound mind in a sound body. Well, can you believe it? I have to help her in and out of the tub and wash her feet for her and she keeps up that damn song and dance about a sound mind in a sound body and how I ought to get myself together. At night, Elly, those reptile age fears come to me. Anyway, Ma and I did sit down together for a talk about the good old days when I would eat a whole head of lettuce all by myself at the age of twelve. And then the tale about the time a man tried to get into the house when Ma left me there alone. He was a genuine mid-Western pervert who probably wanted to assfuck a young boy and then cut his throat. Ma and I hugged each other real close after that story—we might have our differences but we still don't want any physical harm to come to Chucky. So what if my brain has turned to egg white. (*Lights up.*) I'm still able to take a leak and make a phone call every so often. Why don't you answer, Della? What's the matter with you? Do you have cancer? How do you pay your food bills, Della? I'd like to hear you whisper in my ear and say "Hello, Chucky." I was bitten by a woman who turned into a mean green-head fly by the name of Della. Sometimes folks around here see me walking along the road with the moonlight in my hair, carrying a sawed-off shot gun. Guess who I want to find, dear woman? Peggy Guggenheim. Parasite, that's what she is—just a parasitic douche-bag. Hell, I'll never send her one of my bird-feeder constructions. Nope, Peggy's never gonna get a bird-feeder from Chucky. Only lucky Della-Fella will. Dig? I should answer my back door, the handy-man wants to talk about a leaking roof. He's ringing away and Ma's screaming bloody murder because I won't let him in the house. She thinks I was traumatized by the memory of the pervert from years back. Traumatized? Me. Never! The only thing that ever really got me down was the suicides of all our friends. Especially our dear mutual friend, Eugene Ruggles. Well, you can be sure his wife never knew Genie's whereabouts that night. My, oh my, don't I sound like some suburban housewife? I don't mean to be rude, of course, of course. I introduced you to the music of Bach, never forget that kid, you ole rat, you. You were just an unformed baby when I met you. I created you—you Frankenstein monster! Now, I'm the only one who listens to me. I'm a troubador poet. What a fucking place America is. I should have won a Prix de Rome or a Guggenheim. The handy-man is banging away like a crazy-man and Ma's screaming at me to let him in, but I won't. Chucky is not taking any chances, at least not yet. When I answer the door I'm going to have a brick in my hand. How about you, Della, do you keep a brick in your hand when the doorbell rings? Chucky.

(*Lights dim. Taped music of Elvis Presley, "Blue Suede Shoes." Music stops.*)

Dear Lying Eyes,

    How's that for a title of a book I'm going to write? "Dear Lying Eyes." You know the trouble with you is you won't answer any of my letters. What's the matter—are your fingers too greasy to hold a pen? I bet you've become a woman's libber since I went out of your life, Della. But we can always talk about it if you want in some low-down hotel room. How's about it, Della? I'm great at pre-chewing food if that's what you need. No kidding, I can chew your food for you. I do it for Ma. Yup, the woman's bridge broke last week because I accidently smacked her in the mouth with my big carpenter's hand and so I thought that I ought to help her eat by chewing the goddamn food for her so that she can get some nourishment in her. And there's more of an emotional connection chewing up the food than using an automatic blender. Eskimo mothers do it for their kids. I thought I'd try it. How's that for a boy's devotion? Ma doesn't mind. She just looks at me while swallowing what Chucky gives her. I just remembered a little incident years and years ago, in 1960. You and I were strolling along in the Village one sweet summer night, heading for the San Remo, and a bum asked me for some change and for one reason or another, probably because the sonovabitch was too aggressive, I didn't give him anything and he got bittershit and bawled at our backs as we meandered on our way—"You got a woman! You got a woman!" Talk about middle-class values. The fucker thought I should give him some money because I had a woman. Don't put me down, Della. I can still show you a thing or two. The magic christian is still as beautiful as Michelangelo's David. Ma showed me a recipe for chili. I'm going to try it tomorrow. When I put my mind to it I can do anything. After all the suffering Ma has had in her life, to think that her only child, her son, would end up this way. But here I am going off again like a roach out of a crack in the wall. I should cut out the cigarettes, it's making what teeth I have left a very obnoxious green. You used to have strong teeth, Della, big like a horse's. I can visualize you with your big teeth, smiling broadly at me, laughing your head off the way you always did whenever you became nervous. You were so nervous when I knew you. This is for you, Della-Fella. Ma has a bad cough that's not getting better. She insists on smoking up a storm. It's a wonder that she hasn't died of T.B. or cancer. Hah! She'll probably outlive me. Women with their sexual organs are the stronger sex. Dig? I'm pretty sure Ma still gets horny. I know what I'm talking about. And me? I feel like I'm doing myself in but I don't want to do this shitty world any favors—not just yet anyway. Your immortal artist, Charles Craydon. P.S. Elly, when you left me over twenty years ago I bet that you took the big hand-knit Christmas stocking that Ma made to remind you of the old days. I'd like to fill that stocking up with oranges and bars of chocolate and best wishes from your good fairy, Chucky.

(*Lights dim. Taped voice resembling that of a news broadcaster.*)

TAPED VOICE:
The snake and the porcupine had been a couple for five years. Spawned in the woods near Apple Valley, New York, they were a symbiotic entity, cunning, vicious, frightening, above all pragmatic during a killing. In judging this unique duo who liked to play games in the moist muddy furrows near the pond, one had to understand and accept the fantastic attraction the two had for each other; it was something special, ever since the members of their different species had rejected and thrown them out of the home territory for obscure reasons that affront and mock those who hold to current scientific opinion about the unlikelihood of wild animals from different genres forming alliances. This was an extraordinary pair, intelligent and prospering. During that first incredible encounter, the porcupine had dropped seventeen quills to the earth in fright because she had believed that the snake was going to sting her to death. He wanted only to touch her where there were no quills, to rub his length along her voluptuous roundness. With inscrutable thoroughness they smelled each other ravenously. The seasons sailed by and each and every spring struck them as some new wonder of the senses that they had never known before. Together they were rich and glorious, mating, mating always, gasping and hissing in an attempt to beget progeny, meeting each other's opaque gaze in their mutual trance of copulation. The snake and the porcupine did not fear man as the members of their respective species did, although they knew that man caused trouble to the creatures that lived in their midst. There is no more reason to give credence to one theory than to the other—as to why they didn't fear humans, or why they became a couple. One of the most dramatic fights that they had shared together was when they had seized a large husky and began to chew its head and neck so violently that the victim thrashed about wildly in an effort to escape. After the struggling had ended, the pair spent an hour swallowing their prey. All the while a man watched from a nearby bush, showing curiosity and agitation. When the pair made especially violent movements he dashed away in terror only to return again to peer through the bush at the fascinating spectacle. After the meal the couple did a slipping and skidding and zigzagging dance that slowly progressed into copulation.

(*Taped music: West Indian Steel Guitars.*)

Dear Elly,
  I think that yours truly got a bum rap. Not only is Ma complaining more loudly than usual about how bad it is to be old without any grandchildren to make jam and bake cookies for, but also that her very own magic christian son is such a god-awful loser. Yup, one of life's real losers, I yam, I yam. The saddest thing I have to report to you is that my husky, a great big gorgeous animal, kind of like I was when I was twenty, my Freddy, was murdered and

eaten in cold blood by the weirdest twosome I've ever seen collaborating in a killing. Yup. A snake and a porcupine ganged up on Freddy my dog and killed him. I saw it with my own eyes. I bet you're thinking why didn't I scare them off by throwing a rock or something—because my hernia was acting up and I felt awful. And I was in much too weak a condition to defend myself. Anyway, I cried like a baby all night thinking about what happened to my husky.

Ma couldn't say a word to me without my biting her head off. See, I blame her for my hernia because of the Jehovah Witness phase that she went through when I was fifteen, that forbade her to allow me to undergo surgery for my hernia. A simple operation then could have cured me of the damn thing, but Ma's religious scruples prevented me from having it. Is it any wonder that I suffer emotionally as well as sometimes oozing from the fissure in my side from the operation I was forced to have later? Ma's been having grimy thoughts lately—been confiding to me how she has sexual urges and at her age. Eighty-five, God bless her. Says that if only she could meet some nice gentleman at a church social. She begs me to take her to church when she's feeling perky some Sundays. But why should I please her when she wouldn't let me have the hernia operation when I was fifteen? That year when the other boys in the locker room at school found out about my wearing a truss. She could have spared me the pain and embarrassment of the boys' ridicule. I originally wanted to tell you about my dog Freddy's death but I got sidetracked as usual. But do you know any old man who might like to get it on with my mom? He doesn't even have to be a White Anglo-Saxon Protestant. But, I'd better check out her preference first. Ma's still choosy even after having given birth to a snake-in-the-grass like Chucky. Somehow I always felt that I deserved a better name than loser in my life. I mean I had more options than you twenty years ago. I was the one with the superior intelligence and the physical strength. I was the artist and you were just a pretender. But then the female spider does devour the male. Right rubber hammer? How many men have you chewed up, you fat spider? Sign off, bug off, fuck off, jerk off. Chucky.

(Lights dim. Taped music of "Stormy Weather.")

Dear Lost Wonder,

I'm in a slightly gentler state of mind today. Ma did it! Yup. She's got a companion, a boyfriend. No, I'm not kidding. It's true as pimples on a teen-aged girl's derriere. Remember when I told you about Ma wanting a male friend who she could ha, ha, relate to? You know what I mean, Elly, somebody who she could rub her muddy ole body on and maybe chew a thumb or two. Anyway, lemme tell thee what's transpired since. Gee, I feel like I'm telling a fragment of a medieval saga. Here goes. Last Sunday morning, when I went back to the house after dropping Ma off at church, there was a fog over the pond, what some of the older people around here used to call Jack-in-themist. All of a sudden something flashed in my brain. It came to me that something extraordinary was happening that exact moment to Ma right in church. I had this feeling that Ma was very happy at that very moment. Oh, I've had these hunches before. When we were married, I had a hunch the day after we exchanged vows that you were going to leave me. You did leave me too. You cunt. You couldn't stand the fact of being married to an artist. But it's cool. I forgive you kid. Shit I'm digressing from my story about Ma and the old man who maybe I'll be calling Pop one of these days. His name is Chester Nickerson and he's 82-years-old, but if he told you he was sixty-five you'd believe the son-of-a-gun. He's a retired gentleman, to use Ma's words, and he has several children and nine grandchildren, also a nephew who publishes a national magazine. Ma is much happier now that she's found Chester and to tell you the truth, I'm trying to share her happiness. You should see her when she's preparing tea for the two of them, Ma calls it high tea because she serves crumpets in the English manner. She asks me to join them but I know when I'm not wanted—the old bugger is trying to get into Ma's pants. Heh, heh—so I just wander off and leave the two of them alone, but my imagination starts to work overtime and I feel terribly confused because I know Ma doesn't have too many years left and her legs are bad, the old man couldn't care less about Ma's legs looking like broken sausages or all the medication she takes that I'm sure makes her feel horny. Geezus! My brain is popping with pictures, hey, that's a good expression, isn't it? Yeah, my brain is popping with pictures of Ma and Chester Nickerson getting it off together. I know what you're thinking—that they couldn't possibly be making it at their age but that's not true, a person could keep having sex until deep into old age. Why, I expect to make it with room-temperature beef kidneys until I'm fifty-five. Why fifty-five? Because frankly I don't know how much longer I can go on this way, being drunk almost every day, my inability to hold down a job and the affections of my beloved Ma being stolen from me by this dirty old man called Chester Nickerson. And last, but not least, the murder of my dog Freddy. God I miss him so. In a way Freddy was just like a little child, my son, and Ma's grandchild. Don't laugh at my sadness, Elly. God will judge you. Your faithful, Chucky.

(*Lights dim. Taped music of Tango.*)

Dear Della,
 What is happening to me right now is like out of an X-rated film; I'm sure of it as I'm sure of my own name "Chucky Craydon." But it's the circumstances of my life, and Ma and Chester Nickerson, her 82-year-old lover. Yup. It happened yesterday morning when he arrived at the house with his flowers for another one of his long chats with Ma. I decided to join them at tea. During their conversation about politics he began to look in

my direction, a kind of weird stare, and then he'd look at Ma and I could see at once that there was an alliance between them against me. Then out of the blue he announces that the speedometer on his car reads exactly 69,696.9 miles and that was a good number to dwell on and then after saying this nutty statement Ma looks at me with her chin trembling a little and tells me why don't I go into town for the newspaper. I had already made a trip to the dump and I felt like lounging around a little in my own home! Dig? Yes, I know the house is in Ma's name but after her death it's mine! But the way my blood pressure is these days because of all the aggravation I'll probably go first. Anyway, to get back to the point, I tell the both of them that I know they want to be alone and I'll leave to do some work on my new bird-feeder constructions that I've been making. You ought to see them Elly, they're beautiful. Well, I worked a half hour on the bird-feeder constructions and then I thought I'd just slip around to the back of the house outside Ma's bedroom where she and Chester Nickerson are and I'm peering through the gap between the windowshade and the sill and I see that Chester is in the middle of sticking the pink and purple wildflowers that he likes to bring to Ma into her bun on the nape of her neck and Ma is laughing and fiddling around with the zipper of his fly, pulling it up and down in a playful way and then Ma puts her hand all the way in so that it appears that the hand is cut off at the wrist and Chester is sticking his tongue into Ma's ear and then Chester stands up and drops his pants and while still in his boxer shorts that are almost to his knees he pulls up Ma's flowered housedress so that she's sort of trapped temporarily in the armholes and then Chester is unlacing Ma's corset and her breasts which still look, I swear Elly, almost like a woman in her forties, were free for Chester to fondle. I was stunned! I could hardly believe my own eyes when I saw what went on between them. Ma sucking Chester's soft gray dick until it grew hard and then Ma sitting right smack on Chester's face, pulling at his hands with her arthritic fingers, clutching at his wrists while making low groans in the back of her throat. I admit that though I was jealous at what those two had between them, I was also furious and I just hoped Ma wouldn't die of heart failure, or for that matter, Chester. I almost burst out laughing when I saw Ma stick the rim of a small vial of perfume into Chester's asshole. Where on earth did Ma learn her techniques? I wonder that sometimes. They started to fuck with Ma on the edge of the bed and Chester standing in front of her. By that time the noise of their gasping was beginning to sound terribly loud and scary in my own ears and my anxiety was becoming more than I could bear and all I could think of was a glass of cold water and a chocolate nut cookie and being seven years old again. But then I had an image of burning the house down with them inside. And all I wanted really was to get very drunk and be with my dog Freddy who I miss more than this world can ever know. We gave away the puppies and now all I have left is the memory of Freddy. My mother wishes I were dead so that she and Chester Nickerson can be alone together for their remaining years. The feeling around my heart is one of constant pain. The booze offers me some relief but it's all false, just like the values of this world are. Well, I intend to avenge the death of Freddy. I'm going to find and hunt down the deadly duo that took his life. Soon, my quest begins. Until later, Chucky. P.S. Did you know that Ma got a job a month ago stuffing envelopes and I think she's made about $1,000 from an outfit in Daytona Beach, Florida. But I haven't seen one red cent of it. Still another reason that feeds my anger against Chester Nickerson—I bet she gives him the money.

(*Lights up. Chucky is sleeping, head folded in arms. He awakens and sits looking out at audience. Face in shadow. A very deep woman's voice offstage. Taped.*)

WOMAN'S VOICE:
Dear Elly,
   It has been so many years since any sort of correspondence between us, although I did write you a letter about seven years ago which was returned to me for reasons of change of address. Luckily, I was able to get your present whereabouts from the newspapers. I am very happy for you, Elly, that you had a winning ticket in the lottery. Chucky had mentioned it to me, the fact of your luck. This letter that I am in the midst of writing contains some important information that I think you ought to know. My son Chucky has disappeared and there are no available answers to where he has gone or if he is even alive this very day. I know that the fact that you were married to him so many years ago, over twenty to be exact, might lead you to the conclusion that this unhappy circumstance is not your concern, the unhappy circumstance being the disappearance. If you can't follow my line of reasoning, it is because there is no rhyme or reason or constant, orderly line to human life without spiritual convictions. Those smart alecks who are against prayer in the schools are in the upper echelons of the communist party. Anyway back to the premise of my letter and the nitty gritty facts—about two weeks ago Chucky took off about eleven in the morning, it was a Wednesday, to go to the town dump for obvious reasons of refuse removal. We had a huge load of Readers' Digests and old Life magazines dating back to the early fifties, but Chucky couldn't stand the sight of the piles of magazines and papers. I'm certain he got that impatient streak from his father George plus his predilection for drinking. At any rate, since July 5th we have not seen hide nor hair of him. Needless to say I miss my boy very much and lately my mind is filled with memories that only an old woman's mind can be filled with. Memories of when I was a young mother-to-be. I remember distinctly the desire to have a normal child and so I made sure that as soon as I found out I was pregnant, I would never wear a

tight leather belt again that pressed my waist in; now I know, Elly, you always wore tight belts and I'm sure that is why you lost your baby when you were married to Chucky. But these days I think it was definitely a good thing that Chucky never had a child because I'm convinced that the reason for his terrible disturbances are due to the bad genes that he inherited from his father George whom I had to leave because I knew that he would be dangerous to Chucky sooner or later. Oh, I was both mother and father to Chucky as you so well know and as you so well know I would if I had to have gone down on my hands and knees to scrub floors for his college education—fortunately I had a good job as an occupational therapist. I sometimes wonder when I look at the old photograph album of Chucky when he was a child, there are so many pictures of him and me together, why did the misfortunes happen to us? Not you, Elly, you've been doing well over the years. Oh, I know everybody has their troubles but Chucky had a college education. He was such a handsome young man with his dreams about being an artist. Last week was my birthday and Chucky's too. It was a miraculous coincidence that my boy and I were born on the same date. My birthday was pleasant though, I was fortunate to have spent the day with a kind and good friend who I met at church some time ago. A gentleman by the name of Chester Nickerson. He is a widower and is quite serious about remarrying. Chester is eighty-two and in perfect health. We are both of the same Protestant denomination and so forth. He has a whole lot of youthful ideas and can show a man much younger than himself a thing or two about romancing a woman. Chester has a nephew who is a publisher of a nationally known magazine and it is also sold in Europe. They have a fold-out page in each issue and Chester thinks it would be the cat's meow if photos of both him and me were taken in some elegantly refined poses displaying natural love. Of course he's joking but who knows, I cannot see the harm in decent photos of us together. Oh, dear me! I must tell you this information about Chucky's disappearance instead of getting sidetracked as I am apt to do—several days after Chucky's dog Freddy was killed, supposedly by a snake and a porcupine, Chucky kept talking on and on about how he was going to get the "deadly duo" who had taken the life of Freddy. The police and Chester and I theorize that he probably decided to try to find and hunt down the alleged killers of Freddy. They have even put bloodhounds on his trail but have come up with nothing. I'm worried sick over the whole business of Chucky but I've still got to think of practical affairs, like contacting the town refuse dumping service to come and collect my garbage once a week. Chucky used to do that for us—load up all the refuse in the car and take it to the dump. When he'd return I'd always ask him about the magpies and how many there were that day lunching at the dump. The idea of all those birds eating there at the dump just tickled me. Well, I must sign off now. I hope that you are enjoying yourself this summer. Sincerely yours, Marge Craydon. P.S. There was a special prayer service for Chucky offered up by the congregation of the church last Sunday. How I hope all our prayers will be answered and that he will return home safe and sound. Because no corpse has been discovered the police have given up the search and have come to believe that he might have left the area.

(*Lights dim. Taped Japanese non-vocal music. Lights up.*)

Dear Snap-hole, Della-Fella,
   If you took a poll and you dressed up in a black suit, a man's suit that is, you could call yourself Mr. Death. Because like I've told you before and in so many ways—you know all the answers, Elly. So then tell me how I ever found myself in this neck o' the woods. Listen to me, Elly, and like Ishmael I'm going to relate a tale to ye in as high-pitched a decibel as I can make—but like a bat or a porpoise you'll be able to understand what the fuck's been happening to yours truly these past few weeks. For example—what actually was I doing lurking around unfamiliar territory in the first place? Sure I was hunting down the murderers of Freddy—that was my objective. But did I ever consider that I might have experienced an extraordinary phenomenon—and not any mystical bullshit either. Oh come on, Elly, you know what I mean. Don't laugh, I feel—innocent! Yeah, innocent but still the same old nose-thumber as I always have been—and still subject to sexual impulses of a highly erotic nature. Like right now, I'm visualizing you, Elly, wearing high spike heels, your face flushed, erected nipples peeking through your fuzzy angora sweater. Do you know that there are creatures evolving this very second from out of the forest primeval, rodent-like and five-toed with long thick tails, descendants of the saber-toothed tiger? Elly, did you know that Queen Elizabeth the first had a neck shaped like an otter? Oh, if I could only show you all the different and subtle colors of a sea-slug and a squid—then you'd know that I'm still very much an artist. You might think otherwise—that I'm a lunatic. But if I'm a lunatic, Elly, then the president of the United States is a nameless hybrid, a pile of mouse turd. The way the government is treating the people—I'm amazed that the masses haven't risen up in armed revolt! I sound like a communist, don't I? You know, Elly, during the McCarthy era—I helped petition against the asshole. Ah, that's another story. Sometimes, I feel like I've been around since the birth of Christ. At this moment I'm gazing at my sharpened ax, it gleams in the moonlight—in a little while I'm going to follow the scent that keeps drifting to my nostrils, the scent of cotton-tailed rabbit and squirrel which is what I nurture my body on these days, plus some cheap whiskey that I'm able to steal from some hippy now and then. There's a Holiday Inn not too far from where I am and you can't imagine the things they put in the garbage. It makes you wonder about the kind of people at a Holiday Inn. At night while prowling around I'm aware

of tremendous energy, it's during the day that I'm ravaged and exhausted in body and soul—where everywhere I stand is enemy territory—when I flail at the air and let regret wash over me like mud from the river. But Elly, I'm as curious as ever, more curious than a cat or a puppy and for complex reasons these parts of upstate New York fascinate me and there are nights when my wanderings have a clear and urgent purpose as if I'm going to find something or someone that is necessary to the continuation of my being. Your friend, Chucky.

(*Taped Japanese non-vocal music.*)

Dear Above Average Woman,
    Yeah, you are—you know it too. You like the idea also. Being above average. Guess where I am? I'm here under the rocks with the bugs—being watched by the dragons and owls of hysterical imagination. Elly, if I've seen a weird thing—I mean something really weird—I might just chalk it up to being loaded or whatever, but if I see the weird thing again and again, well then I possibly might be correct in my perceptions. Right? Right. You know about the Holiday Inn, well, there are some very peculiar goings-on there. Shit—I want to tell it exactly how I remember. One twilight after I had rescued a nestful of birds from a coupla cats—I heard a din coming from the swimming pool at the Holiday Inn—so I took a look and it turned out to be a gaggle of kids of about twelve—they were riding bicycles around in circles—horsing around the way kids do. I noticed a very lively one who had make-up on his eyes and a leather studded wrist band. He was really a handsome kid. You know a guy like me could really get close to a kid like that. Get your mind out of the gutter, Elly. You know that's not my scene. Anyway, I wanted to run off with the tyke and teach him the ways of an Indian scout—to be silent for hours on end and wait for the fish to bite. And then I saw the kid's father, a bearded guy who wore funny leather pouches snapped to his belt. He was with a dwarf who was wearing yellow loafers. All of a sudden I hear a voice yelling, "Laszlo," and the dwarf turns his big head to look up toward the balcony where the voice is coming from. And standing up on the balcony is an old man—and it's none other than Chester Nickerson. Well, you can imagine what I was feeling at that moment, Elly. But that wasn't the biggest surprise. Oh, no. Because I saw my mom step out on the balcony and she was holding a tall glass of what could have been vodka and tonic and she was wearing a red and yellow gown, and she was smiling. She looked terrific, Elly. I felt my armpits begin to itch. I controlled myself and refrained from screaming bloody murder. Then I see Ma rest her hand on the back of Chester's neck and then he turned to kiss her wrist. I felt as if someone had poured concrete down my throat. I couldn't stand it another minute. I ran away from the Holiday Inn. I went deep into the woods. I felt so **wrong** in the scheme of things. Do you

know, Elly, that the sun is my enemy—a great ball of fire that pours out its hate. I need a colder climate like the Arctic tundra. I used to wonder why the bloodhounds hadn't picked up my scent. I used to wonder that—but now I know. I'm wasted—and the dogs have given up on me. Elly, it's true. And you're so fucking indestructible! Well, I've got news for you—I intend to inherit my piece of the earth. The Rebel, Charles Craydon.

(*Lights dim. Taped music of Italian madrigals. Time passes.*)

Elly,
    I have an image of you in my mind, poking like a finger under my eyelids. You're standing next to a vase filled with wildflowers. My ego is growing claws that are ready to tear off a piece of whatever I can get them into. There is no pattern to my life that you can understand, Elly. I have a hunch, you'll find yourself basking in the sun with me one of these days—but the odds are against it. You'll most likely die in a mental institution at a ripe old age. What do you think of when you look at the old photographs of us together? Do you feel as though you walked away from a head-on collision? I talk to you—you refuse to understand. I loved the way you moved your body—and not once have I pitched woo with anyone but you, dear.

(*Lights down slowly.*)

END

JOHN HAYNES

PHILIP SAYER AND ROBYN GOODMAN IN "A THOUGHT IN THREE PARTS"
["SUMMER EVENING"]

A Thought in Three Parts

Summer Evening

The Youth Hostel

Mr. Frivolous

Wallace Shawn

A Thought in Three Parts was produced by the Joint Stock company (Max Stafford-Clark, artistic director) in London on February 28, 1977, with the following cast:

Summer Evening

DAVID	*Philip Sayer*
SARAH	*Robyn Goodman*

Youth Hostel

DICK	*Jack Klaff*
HELEN	*Stephanie Fayerman*
JUDY	*Robyn Goodman*
BOB	*Paul-John Geoffrey*
TOM	*Philip Sayer*

Mr. Frivolous

MR. FRIVOLOUS	*Tony Rohr*

Director: Max Stafford-Clark
Sets: Sue Plummer
Lighting: Steve Whitson

© 1975, 1982 Copyright by Wallace Shawn.
CAUTION: No performances or readings of this work may be given without the express authorization of the author or his agent. For production rights, contact: Luis Sanjurjo, International Creative Management, 40 West 57th Street, New York, N.Y. 10019.

SUMMER EVENING

David and Sarah, a couple in their late twenties. A pleasant hotel room in a foreign country. A bed by the window, a night table next to it. Sarah is in the bathroom, off-stage, at the start. David and Sarah speak very fast, much faster than people really speak. They almost never leave pauses between their lines, so that their dialogue is almost overlapping.

DAVID: Well dinner was not so bad, in fact. Sarah certainly enjoyed her fish a great deal, which I must say I rather thought was quite a bit better than my rabbit—a hare it was, actually. Hare's quite all right, you know, isn't it, but I would rather have thought that what with scraping the gravy off with a spoon to see the damned thing so that one could try to take out those tiny little bones, I'm not at all sure I wouldn't have done just as well ordering the duck, frankly. Because one couldn't call it filling, or especially delicious, and I'm hungry again, and you see I'll mention it to Sarah. To Sarah. To Sarah. I will mention these things. Now Sarah will hear about my dinner too. Because you see now my friends at home quite like me. My friends at home really do. I'm known as a nice—as a good chap, actually. They find me appealing. But we're traveling here. *(Into the bathroom.)* Sarah? Sarah?—are you feeling at all like some—?—

SARAH: *(From inside.)* What?

DAVID: —I was thinking—

SARAH: *(From inside.)* Just trying things on—

DAVID: —I just thought that we might go down to the—*(Sarah enters.)*

SARAH: What?

DAVID: —to the restaurant and—Lovely dress, love—the—

SARAH: Well? Don't you think just our chocolates, maybe? Do we really—

DAVID: Well—it might be nice—Some sort of a soup, or one of those—
SARAH: Well—I'd rather—my skirt's ripped—
DAVID: Oh really, darling? I was only thinking that maybe some toast—
SARAH: Well then why not go down—
DAVID: I—
SARAH: You probably—
DAVID: —what?
SARAH: You could still get some—
DAVID: What? I know, but I really rather would—what? Did you want to wash?
SARAH: Well no, but I don't see why you—
DAVID: Yes, but then why not—
SARAH: Yes, but—
DAVID: Yes, but then why don't *you* come down too? We could just have some toast and tea and then we could—
SARAH: Well—I really—
DAVID: —you don't feel—
SARAH: I mean, why don't you—
DAVID: —isn't it silly—?—
SARAH: —rather than to bring something up—?—
DAVID: From there? Do you really—
SARAH: Well I don't see—
DAVID: Well all right, I will, but shouldn't—
SARAH: All right.
DAVID: If you're sure that you—
SARAH: Fine. (*He exits.*) Actually, I really would like some toast. I'll tell you frankly I really like toast a lot. I mean, not dry toast, but toast with butter, toast with chicken livers and butter, toast and butter with different kinds of eggs: fried I like fairly well; poached—quite well; buttered toast and scrambled eggs—really marvellous. With that combination, tomato juice. With that combination, orange juice. Orange juice wonderful with ice. I like jam also, like *all* breakfast foods. (*Pause.*) I must say sometimes I rather would like to lie in bed all day and all night and just have tea and toast and jam, if a maid would bring them, I mean. I rather would like to do puzzles, and do little drawings and write little plays to read to myself. And I rather would like to lie there in bed and touch all my toes to my toes and my feet to my feet, and if a crumb of toast by chance would fall from my lips and onto the sheet and find its way down to the bottom of the bed, I wouldn't mind. I wouldn't mind just a bit to spill sometimes my tea, when it's not too hot, or a cold drink too, just to spill those drinks on my bed, and spill my toast on my bed. Now I know that butter is hard to clean off of one's dress and toast is hard to clean out of one's bed and tea and drinks are hard to clean out of one's sheets and bed, but it might be nice just have them in bed there be-

tween my sheets. And I rather would like to splash around quite a bit with that mess in my bed, and kick my legs a bit in my bed, and rub my bottom into my bed. If I needed to pee I would pee in my bed, and my feet would get pretty wet in my bed. (*Pause.*) That's the way I would like it to be when I could read then too—read all sorts of books and papers that I would enjoy. I would keep getting new ones and keep a big basket right near me to throw the old papers in and even old books in. It would need to get dumped out sometimes. I'd dump it myself—right onto the floor, and then I'd kick it about quite a bit. I would rather enjoy to have a sandwich or two in there too to kick about on the floor, and then have some bits of things on my feet as I climbed back in bed and took out my book and tasted my tea and spilled a bit more in the bed. And in the book I would read about people with tea and toast at a table and napkins and glass which would sparkle and glass which would sparkle and cut and shine and people with dresses with jewels, where red and white jewels would be stuck on the clothes. (*Enter David, with a tray of fruit and other things.*)

DAVID: Now darling, I—
SARAH: What?
DAVID: —wasn't able to get what you—
SARAH: What did you get?
DAVID: These are not what we—
SARAH: Oh—well I really don't mind. They seem fine.
DAVID: Well, do they, darling? I'd wanted—
SARAH: They're fine.
DAVID: Oh, I—
SARAH: Yes, they're—(*Silence. They eat. As they eat:*) Yes I'm *quite* content, love—
DAVID: I'm glad, my darling—are you happy, with—?—
SARAH: —how they *find* fruit so ripe—
DAVID: I—
SARAH: —the napkins, and look—
DAVID: —and just always be happy?—
SARAH: —these toothpicks—
DAVID: —and—
SARAH: —starts sort of flat and then round and then comes to a point—
DAVID: Your teeth are so pretty—you bite those things—
SARAH: Do you like my teeth, love?—the saucers—I wish we—
DAVID: I—
SARAH: Wait, though! You still haven't seen my—(*She goes into the bathroom and shuts the door.*)
DAVID: Quietly I watch her dress, undress. Incredible, incredible, she has no idea the trembling in my heart as I lie in bed and watch her clothing, falling to the floor, softly to the chair. (*She enters in a new dress.*) My God—did you

get this dress—today? Your breasts—
SARAH: I—yes—
DAVID: —the color—
SARAH: I was thinking—
DAVID: —that rising—
SARAH: —this top with the very same dress—it seems almost too thin, but I like the arms—
DAVID: —through those sleeves—
SARAH: —it seems—
DAVID: —they slip right through the sleeves—should lie down a bit after eating?
SARAH: Yes—(*They lie down on the bed. Silence.*)
DAVID: You know, there was dancing downstairs—I was really amazed—
SARAH: There was?
DAVID: —the *way* they—
SARAH: Now darling—
DAVID: Don't you find it amazing?
SARAH: Yes.
DAVID: —the way their elbows—those angles—
SARAH: Yes?—
DAVID: And I love that strange music—
SARAH: Yes—
DAVID: —that sort of drunken, that crippled—step—
SARAH: Yes—
DAVID: Oh my love—
SARAH: Am I your love, darling?
DAVID: Oh yes, my love. My love. My love. Do you loathe me?
SARAH: No.
DAVID: But you're feeling—?—
SARAH: What?
DAVID: —in some way?—
SARAH: Why? What? Am I—?—
DAVID: No, but you—
SARAH: What?
DAVID: Would you like that other pear, my love? (*She doesn't reply. He doesn't move.*) No? Well then darling, I think I'll read. (*Pause.*) But you're feeling quite happy?
SARAH: Thank you.
DAVID: You just enjoy thinking? I'll just read quietly and you can think.
SARAH: I'm—
DAVID: Think tragic thoughts, darling?—
SARAH: I'm not thinking, actually.
DAVID: No—well I didn't—

SARAH: I'm not thinking, actually.
DAVID: I didn't—
SARAH: What?
DAVID: —that you *had* to be thinking—
SARAH: Well no. Yes. But I wonder if you do mind terribly my looking out the window? Does it stop you from reading?
DAVID: Not at all, my love—I was only hoping your thoughts weren't tragic—
SARAH: Yes—
DAVID: And now I'm glad that they aren't, my love. (*Silence.*) Yes, it's amazing how *in*expensive the fruit was, in fact, and I really thought it was awfully good.—Didn't you?
SARAH: Yes.
DAVID: This hotel isn't bad—
SARAH: It—No—
DAVID: And the other one really wasn't much less expensive.
SARAH: Well no—not really.
DAVID: You mean, you think it was actually quite a bit less expensive, in fact?
SARAH: Well no, I mean you were right, it wasn't much less expensive at all, actually. (*She gets up from the bed.*)
DAVID: Well that's what—yes—(*She goes into the bathroom and shuts the door.*) Help me. Help me. I want to be bound up and hugged and kissed. Stay with me. Stay with me. Don't stop me. I love you. I—(*She enters in a new dress.*)
SARAH: This one—
DAVID: —that's marvellous, actually—
SARAH: —*inexpensively*, and—
DAVID: Very nice *indeed*—
SARAH: —*incredibly* cheap—yes I will eat that pear—do you want—
DAVID: No, no—Your legs—so lovely, my darling, so perfect—
SARAH: Oo.—just delicious—so sweet—
DAVID: —take the tray out into the hall, I think—I'm afraid of the bugs—(*He exits.*)
SARAH: It's strange, there's nothing, there isn't anything I wouldn't, I wouldn't, I wouldn't do for pleasure. I'd stick a hot poker up my ass if I thought I would like it. (*He enters.*)
DAVID: I love you. I love you.
SARAH: —look cute in that funny-looking shirt, my love—(*She turns up her collar.*)—do you like it like this?
DAVID: Oh yes. Oh yes. Oh yes. It's appealing.
SARAH: Do you find me appealing?
DAVID: I find you—
SARAH: Thank you—
DAVID: —and so terribly light—if you just spread it out—in a breeze—

SARAH: —I'm glad—
DAVID: —with a scarf?—
SARAH: I don't know. (*Silence. He sits in a chair.*)
DAVID: There are so many sounds out there, aren't there?—things in the trees—and people, talking—?—
SARAH: —a festival there by the sea, my love—
DAVID: —a what?—
SARAH: —they're dancing and singing and selling those—
DAVID: —what?—selling?—
SARAH: —those things that they make—with straw, those paper—
DAVID: You mean those hats—?—
SARAH: Oh, they're from a different—
DAVID: Oh, are they?
SARAH: These are—
DAVID: I thought they—
SARAH: These are those things made of twigs, the faces—
DAVID: Oh God, those prune-faced—
SARAH: They've got all the fruit out too—a regular market—oh darling, we—
DAVID: I was wondering—(*Pause.*)
SARAH: Do you like it better buttoned to the top?
DAVID: Let me see it without—
SARAH: Like this?
DAVID: That's nice. I like it.
SARAH: Or this?
DAVID: So nice. (*Silence.*) Do you want to lie down?
SARAH: Why not?
DAVID: Then let's. (*They lie down on the bed.*)
SARAH: A chocolate? (*She takes them from the night table.*)
DAVID: No thank you.
SARAH: Pardon me. I will. (*She eats one, then puts them away.*) I'll just read slightly.
DAVID: Oh, read? Read. That's good. That's good. (*Silence. They read. She slams her book shut.*) Oh, what's wrong, darling?
SARAH: I'm sorry.
DAVID: No, love. No no. That's fine. I'm happy reading here.
SARAH: Well I'm not so happy. I don't like this book. I hate it. I'm sorry.
DAVID: —don't like it?—
SARAH: —not funny, it's dirty—I hate it.
DAVID: I'm sorry.
SARAH: Well it's not your fault—
DAVID: Well it is, I'm sure.
SARAH: Well I really don't think so—
DAVID: I think—

SARAH: You what?—
DAVID: —no, you know, well I feel—Would you like to play cards?
SARAH: No—
DAVID: A short game?—
SARAH: No thank you—
DAVID: I'm only—
SARAH: Yes.
DAVID: —what kinds of diversions—?—
SARAH: I'm quite—
DAVID: I'm just trying to think now—just trying—
SARAH: I'm very very sorry.
DAVID: No, *I'm* sorry—just thinking—are there any other sorts of games with the cards that we haven't ever tried—
SARAH: I'm very, very sorry.
DAVID: Well don't—
SARAH: No?
DAVID: I'm only—
SARAH: I'm—
DAVID: —feel perhaps we might just try to sleep?
SARAH: I'm not tired. I'm not tired. I'm not tired.
DAVID: Well—you mean—
SARAH: I'm tired, but I can't sleep. I can't sleep.
DAVID: Yes, you seem to be sleepy—but are certain fears perhaps—?—
SARAH: Certain fears? But why say that? Do you call it fears when I actually saw an insect as big as my hand in the bathroom yesterday?
DAVID: Did you? Well—but I really wouldn't think that those insects are actually really a danger—
SARAH: Oh no? Well all right, then—you know all about—
DAVID: I don't happen to, no. But I think that we probably might have been told if—it's not awfully likely that *we* were the only ones ever to see—You're not sleepy at all? Yes, it may be because of—
SARAH: But you sleep. You sleep. But I can't. I'm hot. I'm sorry. I'm sorry.
DAVID: Yes. Yes. Of course you were tired before. And I thought that perhaps you might not want to nap, but—
SARAH: Yes well I couldn't really help—
DAVID: Well naps are good, I don't mean that you shouldn't have—
SARAH: What?
DAVID: Well naps are—
SARAH: Really? Really? But you see *you* actually don't need to stay awake just for me. I'm fine. I'm fine.
DAVID: But you don't want to read?
SARAH: Because I just like to sit here and watch all the people, actually.
DAVID: Well yes, but that's fine, and I mean we could both make a trip down

there right now and come back. And I'd really rather like—
SARAH: Well, in fact, you see, I could take a quick trip down there by myself—
DAVID: Yes I mean that you actually do want to go outside—Well then why don't we go? I'll just change my shirt—(*He gets up from the bed and starts to change.*) And I really would like—Did you still want to pee?
SARAH: Well I never said—
DAVID: And I know *you* won't mind if it rains, my love—
SARAH: No I actually rather would like it, in fact—
DAVID: Yes I think I would too, and if our shoes *do* get wet, then we still have those—
SARAH: Yes.
DAVID: —those sandals—
SARAH: Yes—
DAVID: Yes, I *have* been wondering whether actually we *should* have stayed here. It *is so expensive,* and you're right that the heat in these rooms—
SARAH: Well how could you know that you wouldn't in fact have got something worse at the other one, actually?
DAVID: Well—
SARAH: I mean at least here the bathroom—
DAVID: —the bathroom is *great*—I mean, better than—
SARAH: —Yes, well it's fine with me—
DAVID: Well, I'm ready. Well?
SARAH: Well what? Well what?
DAVID: Well—I'm ready.
SARAH: Well—I'm tired. I can't. I can't. No please don't touch me. No. Please. Really. Don't. (*Silence.*)
DAVID: Yes. Well. Fine. You see, I actually had thought, in some way—(*Silence. He returns to the bed.*)
SARAH: Yes. Well I guess you're right, now in fact. We paid a great deal—
DAVID: We what?
SARAH: We paid a great deal, we really paid a great deal for this room which I'd call a pretty ugly little room, I should say—
DAVID: You don't find it attractive?
SARAH: No I really don't think so.
DAVID: Well—it may not be.
SARAH: Well—it isn't.
DAVID: Well—it might not be. Though I rather like it. You see, I rather like it, myself, in fact.
SARAH: Oh, really? Well I rather hate it, myself, you see—
DAVID: —you—
SARAH: Because I don't really like our little lamp very much, and I don't really like our little table very much. And I rather think that that rug there is ugly. And I rather think that that other rug is ugly. And I rather think

that that other rug is ugly. And I rather think that that other rug is ugly. And I rather think that that other rug is ugly. And I wonder—do you like these blankets, David?
DAVID: Well—Yes. I do, actually.
SARAH: Well I don't think I like them, David. I mean they *feel* all right—
DAVID: But the material, Sarah—?—
SARAH: I don't really like that material—no—no—
DAVID: Do you find it in some way unpleasant—?—er—
SARAH: Well, I rather find, yes—oh, I just had a picture, I thought of you strangling me, David—a sort of a day-dream it was, I think.
DAVID: Some sort of a fantasy?
SARAH: And I've actually never thought about choking before. One might get quite queasy, I'd think—
DAVID: Well—really?—
SARAH: —a kind of dizziness—
DAVID: Well?—they say that you—
SARAH: *I* don't mind this sheet, in fact; at least it *feels* rather good—this pillow—
DAVID: Yes—
SARAH: Well, why not hug me, David? You know how to hug me, I think—
DAVID: Would you like to put your head on my chest?
SARAH: I'll put my head—
DAVID: Right there—Quite pleasant—but are some of your bones—?—er—
SARH: No—not really—
DAVID: I feel that your head—
SARAH: No—no, don't move it. That's fine. (*Pause.*) Am I stopping you from reading now, David? Am I?
DAVID: No. Not really. No, I wouldn't say so.
SARAH: Good. I'm only trying to lie here, darling. Not to harm you. Not to destroy you.
DAVID: Good.
SARAH: Not want to destroy you. *Will* you kill me, David?
DAVID: No, my love. No, my sweet. You know I won't kill you. I'll always protect you. Just always protect you.
SARAH: I know that, my darling. And I'll protect you. (*Pause.*) I might just brush my teeth.
DAVID: Well—all right, darling.
SARAH: You find it absurd?
DAVID: Well no, not at all. (*She gets out of bed and goes into the bathroom.*)
SARAH: (*From inside.*) Yes, you see—you believed I never could *brush* my teeth—
DAVID: Well, no—I always—I never—(*She slams the door to the bathroom and returns to the bed.*)

SARAH: And you see, these feelings—these feelings of love and love and love and—
DAVID: What? Do you actually love me, my darling?
SARAH: Well—well—do you know what feelings of love really actually are? Do you know what love means?
DAVID: Well—
SARAH: Or are you actually only a little piece of shit, who's learned how to *talk* about feelings?
DAVID: Well I *feel* that I'm not—
SARAH: But how can you tell?
DAVID: Well I can't tell for sure.—
SARAH: Do you know what love means?
DAVID: Well I can't tell for sure—
SARAH: You can't what?
DAVID: —if I know.—
SARAH: Oh you can't? No?
DAVID: Do you want me to lie, in this case?
SARAH: Well I think that I do.
DAVID: Well then, certainly, yes.
SARAH: Well that's fine then. You know what it means.
DAVID: I'm glad.
SARAH: Well I wish that I did.
DAVID: I'm sorry.
SARAH: I wish that I did.
DAVID: I'm very sorry.
SARAH: Can you tell me something about it?
DAVID: Well it's quite like hatred—
SARAH: Yes—
DAVID: But slightly different—
SARAH: Yes—
DAVID: We don't really want to kill the other.—
SARAH: Yes well that's quite important. Now I think that you're really onto it now—I mean—
DAVID: —well—
SARAH: Love's not killing—
DAVID: No.
SARAH: Or beating?—
DAVID: No. We want to—
SARAH: —putting your penis in my mouth?—
DAVID: Well yes—it could be.
SARAH: Good. Do you love me? David?
DAVID: Oh yes. Oh yes.
SARAH: I once put a silver coin on my tongue. Do you know? Then I dried, I was dripping with sweat. My lips were stiff—yes, the coin was an eye. I was

watching the ocean. The water was black. I was barefoot. The sun stood by me, it was tiny, it was white, it was burning the water. The water was twisting in pain. It was crying. I loved you, I loved you, God damn you fucking shit, freezing horrible shit, you don't care, you fucker, and I'll kill you, I'll kill you—

DAVID: A sticky feeling?

SARAH: —yes—

DAVID: A drippy feeling?

SARAH: —yes—

DAVID: I can see you dead, in a big spotted field. I can see my spot between your shoulder and neck, my field, my own, where I once lay happy, and cool in your shade—

SARAH: You—

DAVID: Now, it's night, there are stars, there are clouds, and they're racing in the sky, and I'm dragging your body by the feet, dirty feet. Your head gets bloody. I'm running. At the end there's a stream, and I lay you down into it and wash you. I stretch you out under a tree, on the grass. I try to suck you, but you're dry and sour. Maybe I'll burn you.

SARAH: David?

DAVID: Yes?

SARAH: Will you leave me tonight, darling?

DAVID: Tonight? What? Will I leave you *tonight*? Here's a book I don't feel like reading. Here's one I don't feel like. Here's one I don't think that I—God, do you hear those sounds? They never get tired.

SARAH: No.

DAVID: But we're always tired. Aren't we, Sarah?

SARAH: Oh no, I don't think so. (*She touches him. Pause.*)

DAVID: Maybe tomorrow we'll buy that dress—the white dress with the flowers—(*Pause.*)

SARAH: —flowers—

DAVID: But why don't you like it?

SARAH: I do. I—

DAVID: —red—

SARAH: Red flowers. White flowers on the white—

DAVID: —stems—pale leaves—

SARAH: —just the light from outside. (*He touches a switch on the night table, and the lights of the room go out.*) Yes. (*They touch.*) Yes.

DAVID: May I?

SARAH: Yes.

(*Blackout.*)

END

THE YOUTH HOSTEL

Two sparsely furnished rooms, not connected, dimly lit, with no windows. Room 1 on the left, Room 2 on the right. Room 1, Dick sitting on the bed, thinking. Room 2, empty. Sounds of birds outside. Long silence before Dick speaks.

DICK: Well—seem to be alone here. Nobody else in. Birds singin' outside. Nothin' much to do—just sit around I guess. (*Pause. Room 2, Judy enters. She turns down the bed, neatens the room, as the scene in Room 1 progresses.*) Fun to play with toys, but don't got none. (*Enter Helen.*) What!? Oh hi, Helen!

HELEN: Hi Dick.

DICK: Aren't you out with the others?

HELEN: Nope. Guess not. (*Pause.*) I guess I'm just different—like you, Dick.

DICK: Yeah, I guess so, Helen. (*Pause.*)

HELEN: Mind if I sit down? I'm feelin' a bit ill.

DICK: Why not. Go ahead. (*She sits down.*)

HELEN: Yeah. My stomach's been gettin' to me. Makes me sick. I hate bein' sick—y'know?

DICK: Yeah. (*Long pause.*)

HELEN: Can you guess what I was doing just before I came in here, Dick?

DICK: No. What?

HELEN: I was doing fuckin' nothing.

DICK: Yeah. That's too bad. (*Pause.*) I hope you're in a good mood now, though, Helen.

HELEN: Well I hope you are, Dick.

DICK: Well, I might be.

HELEN: You stupid ass.

DICK: Yeah.
HELEN: You stupid ass. (*Room 2. A knock at the door.*)
JUDY: Yes—who is it?
BOB: (*Outside.*) Well—It's me—Bob—
JUDY: Oh—(*Pause.*)—Hi Bob!
BOB: (*Outside.*) May I come in?
JUDY: Oh—(*Pause.*)—sure! (*Bob enters.*) Gee Bob—you look all upset. (*Pause.*) What's wrong?
BOB: I don't know, Judy. I guess I just can't sleep.
JUDY: Can't sleep? Gosh—Why, Bob? Are you—too upset?
BOB: No—not exactly. I can't quite explain.
JUDY: You can't? (*Pause.*)
BOB: You see—I'm too nervous to sleep. I'm just too disturbed—
JUDY: Gosh, Bob—
BOB: Can I sit down at least?
JUDY: Of course—I didn't mean—(*He sits down.*)
BOB: You see, I've never had a girl friend, Judy, and—(*Pause.*)
JUDY: I see—you're afraid you just don't know how to talk to girls.
BOB: Yes.
JUDY: Well—(*Pause.*)—I think you're doing just fine right now . . .
BOB: Gee—thanks, Judy. You're the kind of girl a fella might really like to talk to. Really.
JUDY: Well, thank you, Bob.
BOB: No—I mean it.
JUDY: That's nice, Bob. I really appreciate it. (*Very long silence.*)
BOB: Judy—Judy—you know how bad I'd like to touch you.
JUDY: Oh now Bob—don't frighten me like that.
BOB: No, I don't mean to frighten you. But I want so bad just only to look at you—
JUDY: Only to look, Bob?
BOB: I want to see your breasts, Judy.
JUDY: What—naked ones, Bob?
BOB: Yes, Judy. I need to. Really. I won't touch you. I promise. I promise. But I just can't sleep. I can't leave this room. I won't look hard, Judy. But just to look.
JUDY: Bob—I don't know you—
BOB: You have to, Judy. I just can't leave. (*She sits silently for a long while on her bed. Then she takes off her shirt.*) Thank you, Judy.
JUDY: Now will you go, Bob?
BOB: No—I need more, Judy. Your pants too.
JUDY: Oh Bob—please—
BOB: No—I really need it, Judy. I have to see it. (*She slowly takes off her pants. Nude, she sits on the bed so that he can see her genitals. She looks sad. He looks at her*

carefully from his chair.) Thank you, Judy. Should I touch them?

JUDY: No, Bob. (*He stands. Stripping, he approaches her. Then he slowly penetrates her and makes love to her until he comes.*)

BOB: It's not enough, Judy. (*He leaves her.*)

JUDY: No. (*He goes back to his chair.*)

BOB: I expected more.

JUDY: I know.

BOB: Why do you hate me?

JUDY: I don't hate you, Bob.

BOB: I want more.

JUDY: No. Just nothing, Bob.

BOB: Yes.

JUDY: I want nothing.

BOB: Yes. Let's get married, Judy.

JUDY: No, Bob.

BOB: You don't want to?

JUDY: Why should we, Bob? Put on your pants. You'll catch cold.

BOB: Thanks, Judy. (*He picks up his pants, but doesn't put them on.*) I appreciate it. I hate you. But I love you, Judy.

JUDY: I know, Bob. I'm very cold. I'm going to get dressed. (*She puts on her shirt.*)

BOB: Thank you, Judy. I really appreciate it.

JUDY: Let's try to stop now.

BOB: I know, Judy.

JUDY: I'd rather go to bed now. I'd like to sleep.

BOB: I know, Judy.

JUDY: Don't you want to leave now, Bob?

BOB: No, not really—I'll just stay here. I think we'll fall asleep soon.

JUDY: I know, Bob—but don't you think you should leave? I'd like to masturbate.

BOB: I'll watch you, Judy.

JUDY: No, Bob, I could never do it then.

BOB: Get onto the side of the bed, and I'll get on this side, and we'll both do it, and we won't see each other.

JUDY: All right, Bob. We'll see who comes first.

BOB: I'm sure you will, Judy. (*They go to opposite sides of the bed and both masturbate. She comes first.*)

JUDY: That was wonderful. Are you coming, Bob?

BOB: Not yet—now shut up.

JUDY: All right, Bob. I feel terrific—really exhilarated. Gee whiz. Oh come on, Bob—you sure are slow.

BOB: Oh—oh—that helped me! (*He comes.*) Get me some tissues, Judy. I feel like a fool.

JUDY: All right, Bob. Here. Ugh—What a mess.

BOB: Gee thanks, Judy. Give me a kiss. Here—right here. (*He points to his cheek. She kisses it.*) Thanks, Judy. I guess I'd better go. I hate myself—but I'd like to sleep somewhere else.
JUDY: Good going, Bob. I'm going to jerk off some more. So get your ass out.
BOB: Don't be vulgar, Judy.
JUDY: I'm not, Bob. I just love to jerk off. (*He leaves. She lies on the bed and masturbates.*) I really love this. It turns me on. There! (*She moans.*) Ah! Ah! Ah! Oh God—I can just drink that in. Good feelings. Feel goodings. Goo goo. Goo. Goo. Goo. Goo. Jerk jerk jerk. (*Long silence. She lies in bed, but doesn't sleep. Room 1. Helen is wandering around the room. Dick is sitting in a chair.*)
HELEN: (*Playing with flowers.*) I like flowers.
DICK: Yeah.
HELEN: They're really attractive.
DICK: Are they?
HELEN: Yeah. I sometimes feel they're really great.
DICK: Yeah.
HELEN: Why don't we get a few more? Really decorate the place.
DICK: Yeah. Why not? (*Pause.*)
HELEN: I feel so lonely, Dick. Could you hug me a few times?
DICK: Well I really don't want to, Helen.
HELEN: No?
DICK: Fuckin' sorry, but I'm feelin' sort of sick.
HELEN: Yeah. I'll fuckin' hug myself. (*She climbs onto the bed, gets under the covers, and throws her pants out onto the floor. She touches herself under the covers.*)
DICK: You really make me sick, Helen. You really do. I really hate you.
HELEN: Really, Dick?
DICK: You're not the kind of person I like now, Helen. You really aren't.
HELEN: Oh, aren't I, Dick?
DICK: No. You really aren't.
HELEN: Well what sort of person do you like now then, Dickie? Why don't you tell me? I'm really interested.
DICK: Well, people more like Joan, Helen—or people like Alice.
HELEN: Alice? Really? Is she the one you like, Dick? I'll bet she is.
DICK: Well—I do like her, Helen.
HELEN: Yeah—she's really your type. She's really your type, Dick.
DICK: You dripping cunt—will you leave me alone?
HELEN: She's really your type, Dick. Just the type you wet your pants for. Should I tell you all about her, Dickie?
DICK: No.
HELEN: I'll just tell you a few things. I think you'll be interested.
DICK: Go eat yourself, Helen.
HELEN: To start with, sweetheart, her asshole is covered with shit. She's never used toilet paper in her fuckin' life. She's got dirt on her arms up to her elbows. She's a fuckin' liar, and she stole my razor blades twice in a row, and

then she fuckin' hid them—Do you want to hear more of this?

DICK: Go on—why not? What the hell do I care?

HELEN: She eats shit in her room. Wendy watched her. It's not even secret. She'll never do it for me because she knows I hate her, but she does it in front of everybody, all the time. She hasn't shaved her body once since the time she was born, so she looks like a big hairy tree, with big black roots running into the ground. I once tripped her up and stripped off her shirt just to look at her. She looked like a dirty, filthy pig. I pulled down her underwear to look at her crotch, and I was almost sick. It was like a stinking forest growing in all directions. I wanted to look, but she tried to stop me. She stuck her fist in my eye. She almost blinded me. She could have killed me. I tried to smash her head on the ground, but she hit me in the nose, and I was bleeding all over.

DICK: That's great, Helen.

HELEN: Why do you like her so much? Why? Why? Why don't you tell me?

DICK: I don't know. I think she's a decent person. She seems like a good person, like a good person. She's a person, a decent. A person, a person, a decent. I like her. I don't see why you don't like her.

HELEN: Have you ever eaten a meal with her?

DICK: A thousand times. I've always liked it. She's a pleasant companion.

HELEN: Did you watch her eat?

DICK: What do you mean did I watch her eat?

HELEN: I mean did you watch her eat?

DICK: But what do you mean did I watch her eat? What do you mean did I watch her eat?

HELEN: I mean did you watch her eat?

DICK: I don't know what you mean.

HELEN: I mean did you watch her eat, Dick? Did you watch her eat?

DICK: I don't know what you want me to say. I don't know what you want. I don't know what you want. You want me to say things, Helen. What do you want? I don't get it. I don't get it.

HELEN: I said, did you ever watch her when she eats? She doesn't eat the way I think you mean I think I think, Dick. *Now* stop me.

DICK: I'll stop you, Helen, and I mean it. Now you better listen. Now Alice is my friend. A fine person. I want to know her. I do *not* want to see these things, to look, to fight, to get into arguments. We're talking here about my friend Alice, and if you don't like her you can go and drown yourself in shit for all I care, but I don't want to hear these insults and lies. I want the truth.

HELEN: Oh do you, Dickie? You want the truth?

DICK: Yes.

HELEN: You want the truth? Well here it is—your great friend Alice is hated by everyone, including me, and she knows it. Consequently she's taking revenge by making herself disgusting to everbody, and she's leading you off to be a friend of hers so she can make you just like her. She'll catch you off your guard and you'll be eating shit too, Dickie—just like Alice.

DICK: Well well.

HELEN: Yes—that's the truth, baby Dickie. So like it, honey. I hope you like it. (*Pause.*)

DICK: You really get to me, Helen. Yes you do. (*Long pause. In Room 2, Judy gets out of bed, puts on a skirt, and sits in a chair.*)

HELEN: I wish I were dead.

DICK: Is that right? Why is that, Helen?

HELEN: Go fuck yourself, Dick.

DICK: Gee thanks, Helen.

HELEN: "Gee thanks, Helen." You really are an asshole, Dickie.

DICK: Yeah, thanks. Thanks a lot, sweetheart. Why don't you leave me alone?

HELEN: Well why the hell should I?

DICK: Because I want you to. I'm sick of you.

HELEN: Really? Really? (*She lifts up the bed covers.*) Are you sick of this?

DICK: Oh come on, Helen.

HELEN: Come on, Dick. Just finger me, Dickie?

DICK: Why should I?

HELEN: Well why don't you, Dick? Please? Please?

DICK: You're just sitting there, Helen! (*He goes to the bed and fingers her.*) I'll feel your asshole too.

HELEN: Oh God.

DICK: Is that okay?

HELEN: Okay! Okay! Oh! (*She comes. Pause.*)

DICK: Yeah—Well—Look what you've done to my fingers. God!

HELEN: Well—so what?

DICK: Yeah—so what for you (*Wiping his fingers*). You've fuckin' wrecked my whole time, God damn you fuckin' shit—

HELEN: Yeah—Well—Thanks, Dick.

DICK: Yeah—thanks for nothing. Get the fuck out of here.

HELEN: Yeah. Okay, Dickie. See you around.

DICK: Yeah. So long, Helen.

HELEN: So long, Dick. (*Exit Helen.*)

DICK: Yeah. Well. I'm sick to death of these pushy people. What's the point? Do I need that? Why should I care about that? Huh? I'm going to lie right down here and jerk myself off, and if anybody tries to stop me it's their tough luck. That's my fuckin' point of view. (*He lies down and begins to masturbate. Judy leaves Room 2 and enters Room 1.*)

JUDY: Oh, hi Dick! Are you jerking off?

DICK: Well—I *was*. I'm gonna go nuts!

JUDY: But what's the matter? Don't you feel like talking? I thought you'd be lonely.

DICK: Oh Judy—I've been trying to be by myself for hours. Helen's been in here giving me a hard time.

JUDY: Oh—really? Here—let me do it. (*She starts to jerk him off.*)

DICK: No—really—Judy—you really don't need to.

JUDY: I want to—honestly, Dickie.

DICK: I know, Judy, but—

JUDY: You don't want me to? Do you want to have me?

DICK: No—I only—

JUDY: (*Pulling up her skirt.*) Look—here—here—let me get right on you. Oh—oh—you see?—wowee—(*She sits on him, and they make love.*) Oh, boy—this is really enjoyable! Yes! Yes! (*She comes, then he immediately comes.*) Oh, gee—

DICK: Yeah—I have to admit that felt awfully good, Judy. I'm glad you did it to me.

JUDY: Thanks, Dick.

DICK: You've really got a good, sticky hole. It's really a good one.

JUDY: I like you too, Dick.

DICK: But why aren't you out with the others, though, Judy?

JUDY: 'Cause I'm in here fuckin' you, Dick. Now, you know that.

DICK: No, but I mean—

JUDY: No but *I* mean I came here on purpose to fuck you.

DICK: You did? But why, Judy? Do you like me that much?

JUDY: Well—do you really want to know how much?

DICK: Well—how much, Judy?

JUDY: I love you, Dickie!

DICK: What? You do? But what do you mean?

JUDY: From the first time I saw you. You looked really special to me. Different! Really!

DICK: Why Judy! I'm amazed!—Of course I always liked you too, Judy—in those cute little white shorts—you could almost see your vagina—and those downy hairs on your thighs—

JUDY: I knew you loved those shorts, Dick. I only wore them 'cause I knew you loved them.

DICK: God—and to think I didn't know—never even thought you felt anything about me. And here we are! Gosh—isn't it great?

JUDY: Yeah—it really is. Oh God—let's do it some more. (*They make love for a long time and both come. They lie quietly. Long silence.*)

DICK: Judy?

JUDY: Yes?

DICK: You have a beautiful body. I've never seen tits like that—they're so small and petite.

JUDY: I know, Dick.

DICK: I just love everything about you. (*Pause.*) It's dark in here.

JUDY: Yeah.
DICK: There used to be a bear that lived over there. You see?—that spot was some of his urine.
JUDY: Gee, Dick—
DICK: You see, he lived in a kind of forest, with yellow leaves, you see that big red house there . . .
JUDY: Gosh, Dick—
DICK: But you'd better go away now, Judy, though, really. (*Pause.*) I'm beginning to get that sickie feeling again, you know.
JUDY: What, Dick? What sickie feeling?
DICK: I'm beginning to wonder what I like about you, Judy. I'm beginning to feel a bit dizzy—and I don't think I want you here any more—I'm beginning to wonder if you're too thin for me, Judy.
JUDY: Dick—I don't understand—
DICK: No—I really mean it, Judy. You're too thin—your behind—I can't take it, really. Now Judy, please go before I get you now! I'd have to get you, Judy—so get out now! You'd better get out!
JUDY: All right! All right! But you're an odd person, Dick! Why are you odd?
DICK: I don't know! But hurry up and get out of here! Get out! Get out! Now! Now! Now! (*She exits, leaving her skirt behind.*) I'm mortified. I kicked her out just like a dog. But what could I do! I hated her! She's just not healthy! When I saw that behind, like a pushed-in face—No! No! I really could have killed her! My God! My God! And she was so good-looking—that wonderful vagina, those breasts—dark and tiny! I loved them so much! But I felt too angry. God—God— it's so hard to keep in charge. It's so difficult. (*Pause.*) Oh God,—God,—tired's not the word. I need such a rest. A rest, very quiet. Lots of swimming. (*He masturbates, making sounds. He comes, with more sounds.*) Ah—That was great. Good orgasm! God—I really needed it. (*Pause.*) Wow. Now I'll close my eyes. Boy oh boy. Sleep. Sleep. Coming. Soon. Good. Here. Goo. (*He sleeps. Judy enters, looking for her skirt.*)
JUDY: I'm sorry, I left my—Hey, he's asleep! (*Pause.*) God, he doesn't look so frightening now! Hi, sleepy-head—where'd you put that thing? (*Enter Helen, in a skirt and top.*)
HELEN: Oh—hello there, Judy.
JUDY: Well—well well well! Hi, Helen!
HELEN: Hi, Judy.
JUDY: Have you come to see Dick? He seems a bit grumpy.
HELEN: I think he's sleeping, Judy.
JUDY: Yeah.—Well.—You know what I mean. (*Pause.*)
HELEN: Yes, I've been feeling a bit bored, you know, lately, Judy—
JUDY: Uh-huh—
HELEN: And I thought I might visit a little penis he has, you know?
JUDY: Oh—Really? Why not visit mine, Helen?

HELEN: That's very funny, Judy. (*She lifts Dick's blanket and puts her head under it.*) Let's see who's here. Hello? Hello? Does he have one in here, somewhere, d'you think? I can't seem to find it. (*Judy lifts up Helen's skirt and puts her head under it. Helen shrieks.*) Oh God, that tickles! (*She pulls away, laughing. Judy follows her, laughing wildly. Helen climbs onto the bed to escape. Judy climbs on also. Both are laughing wildly. Dick wakes with a start.*)

DICK: Hey! What!? What!? What the—

JUDY: Hi there, Dick! Just grabbing a little bite here—(*She rips Helen's skirt off and starts to suck her. At first Helen fights her, laughing wildly, but then she relents. Dick watches them.*)

DICK: Hey—how's she doing there, Helen?

HELEN: Well I'm not too sure. (*Pause.*) She's really a pig. Ow—come on now, Judy!

DICK: Is she really that bad?

HELEN: Oh really, Judy! Really! Really! (*Judy looks up.*)

JUDY: What's wrong, you shit?

DICK: You cunts. How disgusting.

HELEN: You made him grow a penis there, Judy. See?

JUDY: Hey, I think I like that. (*She starts to suck Dick's penis.*)

DICK: Hey! (*Dick starts to laugh loudly.*)

HELEN: You like that, huh, Dick.

DICK: She's not bad at this, Helen! (*He is laughing wildly. Helen is looking for something.*)

HELEN: Where is that fuckin' thing? (*She finds a dildo and begins to masturbate with it on the bed, while Dick continues to laugh. Finally he comes. Helen continues masturbating.*)

DICK: Not bad, Judy.

JUDY: Hey, look what she's doing.

DICK: Hm . . . Rather appealing.

JUDY: Thinks she's pretty clever, I can certainly see that. (*Helen comes.*) Can I borrow it, Helen?

HELEN: Go eat your titties, Judy.

JUDY: Why not? (*Helen begins to masturbate again with the dildo.*) Oh come on, Helen. Why not? (*Helen ignores her.*) Why not?

HELEN: It's really something—(*Judy rushes at Helen, as if to grab the dildo, but Dick pushes her away.*)

DICK: Get out of here, Judy. Come on, get out. (*Judy yells at them.*)

JUDY: You disgusting pieces of urine!! (*She goes out, slamming the door. Helen masturbates more and more vigorously. Dick gets out of bed, goes to a big box, takes some food out of it, and eats it. Enter Bob.*)

DICK: Hey—hi there, Bob.

BOB: Hi, Dick—My God—what she's doing!—

DICK: You like that, Bob?

BOB: You're naked, Helen—I can see your—(*Pause.*)

A Thought in Three Parts 51

DICK: Do you like that, Bob old man?
BOB: Oh God, gee—I can hardly stand this, Dick. I can really see in there. Every part of her vagina. What she's doing—what she's doing—(*She comes, lies exhausted for a moment, puts down the dildo.*)
HELEN: Oh. God. Well hi there, Bob.
BOB: Hi, Helen.
HELEN: Hi. Hi hi.
DICK: Well go ahead, Bob. You want to jerk off, you just go ahead. We won't stop you. (*Dick returns to the bed.*)
HELEN: He wants to jerk off?
DICK: Well, don't you, Bob?
HELEN: (*To Bob.*) Yeah, we can't stop you. (*Pause.*)
BOB: Really? Really? You mean you want to see it?
DICK: If you want to show it. (*Bob takes out his penis.*)
BOB: See? Look.
DICK: It seems all right.
HELEN: Yeah. It looks like a penis. (*Bob is sitting on the bed with Helen and Dick. He masturbates. Helen and Dick watch.*)
BOB: (*Masturbating faster and faster.*) I'm coming soon!
DICK: Oh boy.—
HELEN: Oh—God—
BOB: Oh! (*He comes, shooting sperm toward Helen and Dick.*)
DICK: Whoops—catch!—Yuck. (*Helen is laughing hysterically.*)
HELEN: (*To Bob.*) You're such an asshole! (*Laughing.*)
BOB: Oh wow—that was good—
HELEN: Yuck! Yuck! What an asshole!
BOB: Well—why not? Can you equal me, Dick?
DICK: Can I what? What?
BOB: Well—can you?
HELEN: Yeah, Dick. Let's have a little contest. Let's see how you do. (*Pointing to either side of her.*) Now you sit there, and you sit there. And now here's my pretty little belly, and my nice little tits, and my cute little neck. Now aim this way, and let's see who gets higher.
DICK: Oh come on, Helen.
BOB: Yeah, let's see it, Dick.
DICK: Are you really serious?
HELEN: Come *on*, Dick! Stop wasting our time.
DICK: Well come on, Helen! I don't think I'm in the mood.
HELEN: I hate him! I hate him! All right, I'll start you. (*She kisses him until he starts to laugh.*)
DICK: Okay! Okay!
HELEN: I really hate you, Dick. (*Bob and Dick both start to masturbate.*) All right then, come on boys. Let's see a little speed. Let's go. Let's go. Let's go!
BOB: I'm closer—oh God—(*Bob comes. Then Dick comes. Silence. Then Helen*

speaks.)

HELEN: Boy, I'm feeling pretty wet up there, Bob. I'm really soaked.

DICK: Well I thought mine was higher.

HELEN: Oh come off it, Dick.

DICK: Well—wasn't it, Bob?

BOB: Well you did pretty well there, Dick, but I thought mine was up to her face.

DICK: You what?

BOB: Think I'll try it again.

HELEN: Could you aim for my mouth?

BOB: Well there's no harm trying. (*He starts to masturbate.*)

HELEN: Well come on then, Dick.

DICK: Go suck yourself, Helen.

HELEN: Well come on, Dickie! Don't wreck everything! Come on! Come on! (*She touches his penis.*)

BOB: No fair! Dammit!

HELEN: (*To Bob.*) You shut up and keep working. (*After a while, to Dick.*) You're getting no place, Dick. You're just pathetic. (*She removes her hand.*)

DICK: You're a shit-head, Helen. (*Helen starts to masturbate with the dildo. Dick watches her for a long while. Then he speaks.*) I said you're a shit-head. (*He grabs the dildo and throws it across the room. She tries to run to get it and he grabs her and wrestles her down to the floor and starts hitting her. Grunts and cries. Enter Judy. Bob keeps masturbating.*)

JUDY: Hi there, Bob.

BOB: Hi, Judy. I'm just doing this.

JUDY: I can see that, Bob. (*She looks at Helen and Dick.*) Those disgusting farts. (*To Helen.*) I'm taking your little thing, you disgusting vomits. (*She picks up the dildo and licks it. Dick and Helen stop fighting for a moment to look at her, and Helen rushes at her, pulling her to the floor by her hair and hitting her. Dick tries to pull Helen off, and all fight violently. Judy is screaming. She still holds the dildo. Then Bob comes, dripping sperm over them, and they stop fighting and separate. Silence for a moment.*)

HELEN: Oh, wow—

DICK: God, thanks for the sperm there, Bob. (*Judy is sitting at some distance on the floor from the others. She begins to masturbate with the dildo, more and more vigorously.*)

BOB: Gosh, what a wonderful feeling. I love the way it feels right here, just right at the edge. (*Pointing to the head of his penis.*)

HELEN: Hey, my hand is bleeding. (*Judy finally comes and drops the dildo on the floor.*)

BOB: God, it's freezing in here. I hope we don't catch cold! (*Exit Judy. Suddenly all feel cold. Bob sneezes loudly, takes a blanket and wraps himself up. Judy enters Room 2 and lies down on the bed. She masturbates with difficulty, manually and with *her pillow. Bob leans against a wall of Room 1 and shuts his eyes. Dick washes himself with some water in a corner of the room and finally lies down on the bed. Helen wraps herself in a blanket and gets some food from the big box. She eats it, huddled to the wall. All are shivering. Judy continues to masturbate.)*

JUDY: It's so unfair. Just so unfair. (*Judy comes, and then sleeps. Long silence. In Room 1, Bob and Dick fall asleep. A long, long silence. Then Tom enters Room 2. He switches on a rather bright light and kisses Judy.*)

TOM: Hi, darling.

JUDY: Hi, Tom. (*Waking up.*)

TOM: How's my sweet little wife?

JUDY: Am I your wife, darling?

TOM: Of course, my angel. You remember that.

JUDY: I know, Tom.

TOM: I've brought some breakfast. I sure could eat it.

JUDY: So could I, Tom. I'd really love to.

TOM: Here. Fix it yourself. However you like it.

JUDY: Thanks, Tom. That would really be great. (*She fixes the breakfast and they sit at a table and eat it.*)

TOM: Smells like sperm in here, Judy. Did you have visitors?

JUDY: Only Bob, darling. He made me do it.

TOM: Bob? He's crazy! I think he's odd—I almost do.

JUDY: He is odd, darling. A peculiar person.

TOM: Does he love you, darling?

JUDY: I don't know, Tom. Sometimes I think so. I wish *I* were odder.

TOM: I know, darling—I guess it's difficult.

JUDY: Do you think Bob loves me?

TOM: I'm not sure, sweetheart. He certainly seems to.

JUDY: I'm glad. I like him. I think he's nice.

TOM: Don't you like me, Judy?

JUDY: Yes, but he's nice too.

TOM: I know, darling. I was only teasing.

JUDY: All right, Tom. I knew you were. (*Pause.*) Have some more food.

TOM: Thanks, Judy. (*Silence.*)

JUDY: Tom—do you think I ought to wear trousers, darling, or just a dress?

TOM: I'm not really sure. Do you want to wear trousers?

JUDY: Yes—I think so.

TOM: Well—why don't you then?

JUDY: Well all right, Tom. Thank you, darling. (*She dresses.*)

TOM: I ran into Baby Naylor last night. He's playing trumpet with Leiku Kanefian.

JUDY: Really, darling?

TOM: Yes—that's what he said.

JUDY: That's great. How nice. What a good position! (*Pause.*) Gosh, Tom, I

wish *you* had a job. Why *don't* you get one? You know you're qualified.
TOM: I know, Judy. But I just can't concentrate.
JUDY: Does your mother support you, sweetheart?
TOM: You know she does, Judy.
JUDY: I guess I thought perhaps she'd stopped it, Tom.
TOM: But why would she stop it, Judy? That's silly. You know she cares about me.
JUDY: I know that, Tom. I certainly know that, my darling. I know that, baby. I know. I know. I do know that, darling. I know, darling. I know, darling. I know, darling. I know, darling.
TOM: I know you know, Judy. I know that, dear. (*Silence.*)
JUDY: Bill—
TOM: I'm Tom, darling.
JUDY: I know you're Tom, sweetheart. I was just talking to you.
TOM: I know, darling.
JUDY: Tom—don't you think we should clear out some of our odds and ends, darling? Our possessions have accumulated so. There are so many things we don't even need.
TOM: Or want. That's true. Really. Let's chuck them all out.
JUDY: But Tom—don't you like our things?
TOM: Well—I don't know, darling. Not really too many. They're mostly junk, after all.
JUDY: Well I guess so, darling. I picked them carefully.
TOM: Well—all the same. I think they're junk.
JUDY: I guess you're right, Tom, and we'd better chuck them.
TOM: Okay, Judy—if you want to.
JUDY: If I want to?
TOM: Well—it was your idea.
JUDY: Well—I suppose it was, darling, but it was really your idea.
TOM: Well, I suppose it was, darling, but it was really your idea.
JUDY: Well, it was really your idea, darling. But let's get them out. (*Silence.*) Tom?
TOM: What?
JUDY: You're in a bad mood, sweetheart. What's the matter?
TOM: I'm sick of my job. The goddamned boss gets into my hair.
JUDY: But what job, Tom?
TOM: He crosses me every chance he gets. Damned son of a bitch.
JUDY: You don't have a job, Tom. I wish you did.
TOM: Well so do I, dammit. Why are you stopping me, then?
JUDY: I'm not stopping you, Tom.
TOM: You liar—don't you say you're not stopping me.
JUDY: Don't say it, Tom?
TOM: I said, don't say it. (*He slaps her.*)
JUDY: Okay, Tom. You win. You win.

TOM: You bet I win, baby. That's what winning's all about. (*Long silence. Then he hits her again. They fight violently on the bed. Long silence. In Room 1, Helen shifts her position against the wall, still cold and shivering. Long silence. Tom is almost asleep. Then Judy gets up, touches her face.*)
JUDY: Very interesting. Tom, you know you've wounded me. You've really harmed me.
TOM: What?
JUDY: I say, you've really harmed me.
TOM: I have?
JUDY: But not too interested?
TOM: I thought I was sleeping.
JUDY: I think you're an asshole, Tom.
TOM: I thought I was sleeping.
JUDY: Are these dreams, Tom? I really feel bruised. These welts really hurt. You've finally hurt me, Tom.
TOM: "You've finally hurt me, Tom."
JUDY: Do you like me, Tommy? Do you really like me?
TOM: Your mouth is open, Judy.
JUDY: Do you really like me? Do you really like me?
TOM: I know what it means, Judy. Put on more makeup?
JUDY: "Here we finally are, Judy."
TOM: Do you want to help me now? I could use a fuck.
JUDY: "I think I understand you, Judy." (*They sit for a long time. Both feel cold. Judy shudders. Silence.*)

END

MR. FRIVOLOUS

An appealing room. Mr. Frivolous, a man in his early thirties. Breakfast on a table. Mr. Frivolous is about to pour some coffee for himself.

MR. FRIVOLOUS:
Mmm—yum yum yum—now for a good cup of coffee. (*The coffee spills.*) Whoops. (*Pause.*) I guess it—yes. (*He wipes up the spill.*) The birds outside always twitter. And the leaves!—heh heh. Now don't make a mess. Yes. (*He pours the coffee again and sips it.*) I always ask these mornings why, I always ask why the creatures flutter by the curtain just as the sun dips, behind a cloud. Darker, darker. They're so loud—they might be in the room. Right here on a branch. (*Pause.*) I ask the little bird why he stays, and he flies, away. I ask him why he cries, and he sighs. He asks why wait, why not fly, now, down, to the water, to that bubbling water, down by the sand. I ask. He asks. (*Pause.*) What a terrible breeze. It's cold and cloudy. (*Pause.*) Daisies. Sweet flowers. I step on a threshhold of grass, a stair of grass, running with water, a glassy platter streaked here and there with a cellophane, taped, tasting, a berry. I stand on the water, my shoes barely wet, with trees on each side, passing, with clouds dark with rain, waiting to pour.(*He looks at the food on the table.*) I don't feel like this. Let's get this stuff out of the way. Now. (*He moves the food.*) Tired. Yes. And a little bit sick. I'm sorry. You don't find it appealing. I'm sorry. I'm sorry. I'm sorry. I'm sorry. (*Pause.*) I've asked you once, who flies with the crow. Where do they both go. Why the sky is grey where the crow flies, why I'm tucked in the corner of his wing, a pilot, watching the earth, like a jewel on a ring. Dogs are mating outside. Come into the garden. You can see—there. Lettuce, you see dirt. Just a few little flowers. (*Pause.*) And I wonder, who are you, the darling, what are you? Your face comes to me, I

hold you, my diary, my pouch, my pocket. I'm awakened by a late-night telephone call, make my way from bed, to my robe and a cushion, to speak, to you. The room is cold. And you too lie in darkness, far, from me. I say, "When I open, the blinds, in the morning, the particles, of dust, sparkle. There are curtains, on the windows, and a bird, outside. A bird. I sing, as a bird." I ask you to love. I ask you to love me. I ask to be taken, out to the toilet. And washed. And cleaned. And washed. And cleaned. I ask. I ask. I ask. I ask. For your arms. To be there. And your shoulders. There. And for you. To open. And for you. To hold. To take. Me in. To hug on me. Hard. While I. Am sliding. While I. Am pressing. While the hours. Pass. And our bodies get wet. Our bodies get slippery. And cold. And cold. And cold. And cold. These truths, beam fresh, to me, tonight, with the moon, coming in, my window, as I speak. Come get me, come find me. I lie here naked, I lie here waiting. Now. Now. Now. Now. I want, to be pulled, and looted, and ripped, by your nails, and strangled, with your stockings, and painted, like a placard, with your lipstick, on my back, on my legs, on my ass, on my asshole. And these things, these, lying around—these sheets, these bits, of clothes, of brassieres, of panties—I think, these are an easel, for all that work. (*Pause.*) Then I speak, to my priest, and I say, Priest, touch me. Priest, Father, I have asked you to come here, to tell you, these clothes of yours have stayed here with me too long. Lie down here beside me. (*Pause.*) Precious are the priests who lie by the side of their lovers. Precious are the priests whose arms touch the arms of lovers, whose prickly cheeks touch the face of lovers. (*Pause.*)

> Let us get up now, quickly, and grab our robes, thrown under the chair,
> and open the cold, cold windows to clear the air,
> of the smells of passionate love making there,
> and then go to the bathroom and wash our hair.

(*Pause.*)

With wings unfurled, our angels scattered light across the grass. We waited while they did, and then ran back to us, and sent them out, again. You, the littlest angel, ran under my robe and held my legs. At dawn, we saw the sun begin to tip the leaves and chase out and wring out the drops of dew. We watched while the light began to firm the trunks and sharpen the twigs and branches to a point. Then we gathered up our clothes, long since discarded as we lay in the grass, and headed for home, to wash, to dress, to have dinner, and then to bed, and tuck you in, and lights out.

END

JOSEPH SCHUYLER

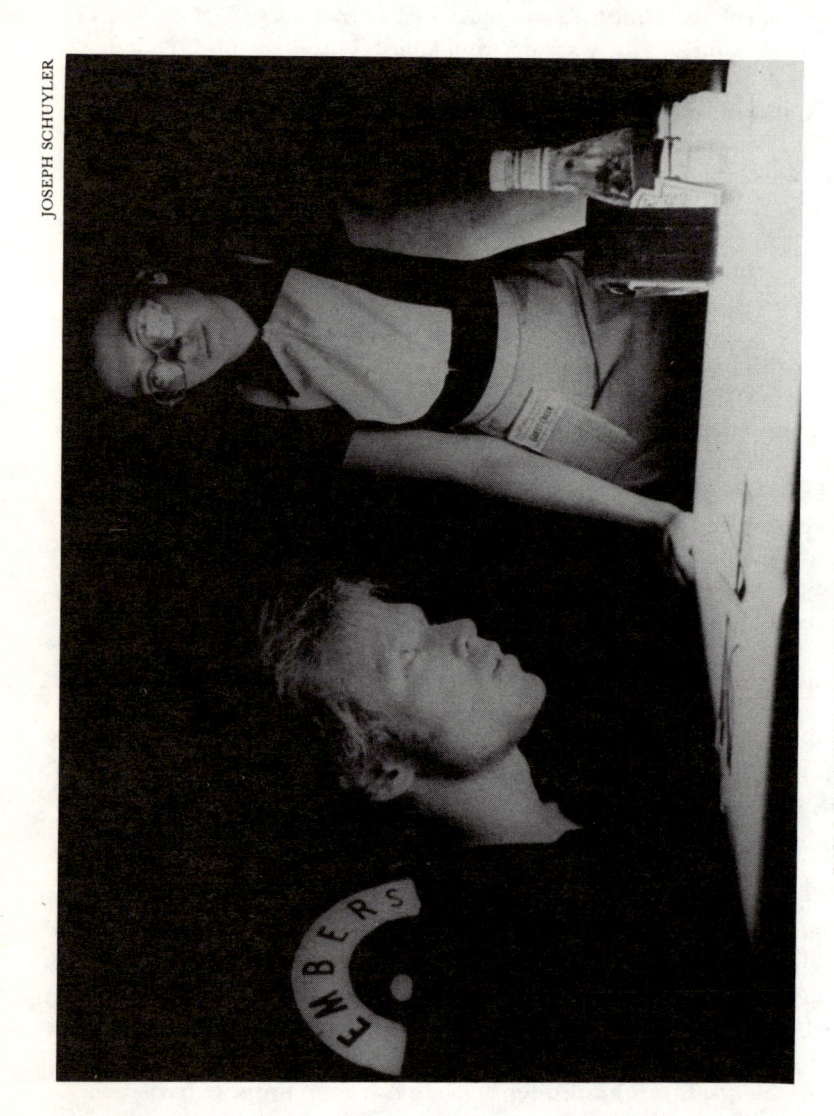

WILL PATTON AND BETTY LAROE IN "DARK RIDE"

Dark Ride

Len Jenkin

Dark Ride was produced by Soho Rep (Jerry Engelbach and Marlene Swartz, artistic directors) in New York City on November 13, 1981, with the following cast:

TRANSLATOR	*David Brisbin*
MARGO	*Melissa Hurst*
JEWELLER	*Bill Sadler*
THIEF	*Will Patton*
WAITRESS	*Betty LaRoe*
GENERAL	*Eric Loeb*
ED	*Walter Hadler*
EDNA	*Saun Ellis*
MRS. LAMMLE	*JoAnne Akalaitis*
ZENDAVESTA	*John Nesci*

Director: Len Jenkin
Sets: John Arnone
Costumes: David C. Woolard
Lighting: Bruce Porter
Sound: Kathleen King
Projections: Gerald Marks

© 1981, 1982 Copyright by Len Jenkin.
CAUTION: No performances or readings of this work may be given without the express authorization of the author or his agent. For production rights, contact: Flora Roberts, Inc., 157 West 57th Street, Penthouse A, New York, N.Y. 10019.

ACT I

1.

Ride in: light, sound.

VOICE: Listen lady. If he's old enough to enjoy the ride, he's old enough to need a ticket . . .

2.

TRANSLATOR: My translation of the Book of the Yellow Ancestor is progressing very poorly. Ever since I began the work for this publisher of occult esoterica, I've suspected that something was seriously wrong. Possibilities: the text submitted to me was claimed to be a xerox copy of a parchment recently discovered in a cave in Szechuan Province, near Foo-Chow. How this document came into the possession of Mr. Zendavesta of Sublime Publications he did not say. His response, when queried, is a genial grin. It is possible, then, that this text is fraudulent, or, if genuine, extremely corrupt. Either one of these theories is true, or—I'm somehow no longer able to make modern English sense out of ancient Chinese. In all honesty, with this text, it sometimes seems that I can no longer even read the language—brushstrokes seem like chicken scratchings in the sand.

Yet the Book of the Yellow Ancestor is definitely not composed of the kind of subtle or paradoxical discourse that could trouble the translator. Still, my tentative drafts all feel wrong—not nonsense, but *off* somewhere, at some angle . . .

I better explain. Actually, this Book of the Yellow Ancestor is not a book. It consists of one hundred and one fragments, which I assumed at first to be pithy phrases about life, or a set of directions for spiritual practices. Now I am not sure but that it is actually the journal of a housewife, equivalent to a laundry list, or the pointless travel diary of a garrulous lunatic, or a series of instructions for operating some partially biological machine that no longer exists.

The work of translation, as you might imagine, is confusingly dependent on my changing notions of these contexts.

Well, whatever the cause, there seem to be major blocks in the way of progress.

That's an understatement. The truth is that certain sections of the manuscript make me almost sure that either it's a modern forgery, or that I'm going crazy. There's even one fragment . . . let me find it here . . . Ah—I've worked this passage over a dozen times, and it persists in coming out the same way. It seems to be describing a young woman reading some sort of popular novel. I quote. "Margo lies back on the couch in her apartment, and opens a book. She turns the pages slowly, until she finds her place. Her lips move slightly with the words she reads, like a child. . . ."

3.

MARGO: Chapter Nine. At the Clinic. The man in bandages stands up slowly and walks over to the window. The sunlight is bright, and perhaps a ghost of it filters in through the layers of gauze that cover his face. But there's no need to speculate. Actually the light is felt by the man in bandages as heat . . . nonspecific. He translates it into whatever suits him: this morning, a certain theatre in flames. Once his facial parts are sufficiently warm, he speaks to his visitor, a figure in white.

JEWELLER: I'm Ravensburg. I remember you, your voice, the smell of your hair—from long ago—or from a dream. I've dreamed every night since they brought me here. Who are you?

MARGO: The figure does not answer.

JEWELLER: He has robbed and beaten me. These bandages come off tomorrow, and then . . . WHO ARE YOU?

MARGO: Ravensburg says suddenly, with an unusual amount of emotion. The man in the next bed groans.

MAN: Unnnhh!

MARGO: Ravensburg continues.

JEWELLER: Here at the clinic they've treated me well. After the operation, they offered to spice my recuperation with all sorts of improvements. They offered plastic surgery, external realignment to go along with what they'd done inside, but I wanted to keep the scars. But you? What about you?

DOCTOR: Ah, there you are, number ten. You know you're not allowed out of the ward. Nurse—is anyone else disturbing the others?

MARGO: Enough book. Record player. (*Music.*) Stories about mental illness make me nervous. I keep thinking I'm a nurse at this clinic. It's actually a small sanitarium in the mountains. I'm a minor character who has her own little life . . . a boyfriend, a bicycle, a little house in the village . . . and I receive the major dramatic events, not in a direct and concerned way, but from a distance, like I'm overhearing two people I'll never see again, while I'm doing something else. Crazy, hah?

I've been jumpy since my boyfriend disappeared. Three weeks ago, he went out to sell something he found on the street—he finds things all the time—but he never came back. I thought he was dead or something, and I called every precinct, and then I called the hospitals.

Nobody ever heard of him. So I'm like a war bride or something, and then I get this postcard with a picture of some guy I don't even know on it. Can you believe it? "Dear Margo, I can't say where I am cause there's some people probably looking for me."

THIEF: I ran into some good luck and some trouble. I'll send for you.

MARGO: Send for me. He didn't even sign it, and I'm supposed to give up my job and go someplace? I can hardly stand living with him here where I got people I know. So now he's gonna write me from Cloud Cuckoo Land and say come on out the weather's fine. Pack your ermines, Margo. I love him but it's stupid, you know, like we have no idea how to love each other but we love each other anyway so we try but it comes out stupid.

Well, I've been nervous. I've been feeling that wherever I am, a certain someone else has been there just before me. Crazy, hah?

This card is postmarked, Indianapolis, Indiana. You know what I think of when I think of Indianapolis, Indiana? . . . It's like it reminds me of something that's not it . . . some other place that I don't particularly want to dream about . . . outskirts of some city, for miles alongside highways, feeding out into suburban streets. . . .

4.

THIEF: Outskirts of some city, for miles alongside highways, feeding out into suburban streets, and I'm walking, and I keep looking back over my shoulder to see if anyone's behind me. I have the damn thing in a leather bag around my neck, and I'm heading south, and I figured I better . . . after three days on the road, I figured I better get inside somewhere, I figured I better eat something. I'm in America, coming into town. There's these long stretches of seedy apartment houses. Some people on the steps of one of them with a baby, and they're drinking beer, and they say hello out of the dark, and they don't even know who they're talking to, you know, but I say hello back anyway, and that seems to be it 'cause I just keep walking and they don't say anything else. O.K. Now I'm really hungry but it's a long way between neon, and then I see one coming, a red blur in the distance, and I squint at it, wanting it to say *Café* or *Eat Here* or something, but it ends up saying *Tri-City Furniture* or *Red Robin Autos*—Used But Not Abused—and finally I see another one, and it's a revolve, turning and turning, and it says *The Embers. We Never Close.* So I go in. I'm here. Jukebox.

WAITRESS: Please wait to be seated.

THIEF: I'm seated. I'm in a chair at this table with this sugar and salt and pepper and a napkin and silverware—And I make sure the bag is hidden under my shirt. I got a menu, and I'm reading the section entitled: Burgers. Embers Burger—bacon cheese and tomato with our special sauce. Burger Hawaiian with zesty pineapple. Burger Royale . . .

WAITRESS: You know what you want?

THIEF: Uh . . . yeah. A Burger Royale.

WAITRESS: Anything to drink?

THIEF: Yeah.

WAITRESS: What?

THIEF: Coffee.

WAITRESS: (*To kitchen.*) Burger Royal.

DEEP SEA ED (COOK): Burger Royale.

THIEF: I'm still reading the menu to see if I made a mistake—Baked meat loaf Viennese, mashed potatoes, mushroom sauce. Vegetables du jour: carrots and peas, cauliflower, creamed corn . . . and this guy comes out of the kitchen wearing this white apron, and he slides into the seat acorss from me.

ED: Hello, slick.

THIEF: He says.

ED: Got a cigarette?

THIEF: I give him one and he says

ED: Thanks. You new here?

THIEF: Then I just look at him, and he looks back at me, and then he goes away.

I can see the TV, over the bar alongside the dining room. The waitress flips it on. It's in funny color like the tint knob's twisted, and she's tuned in to Outer Limits. O.K. I like that. Then she changes the channel.

Desert wind, billows of sand, straggly barbed wire. Zoom in past a dead camel covered with flies . . . on to a tattered tent. Inside, at a table covered with maps, sits this man in some kinda uniform, and he looks right at me. . . .

5.

GENERAL: Serving as field commander for a senile and capricious ruler is a thankless task. You are blamed for everything, though you simply follow orders. If you fail to develop the psychic strength necessary to deal with the intense and often obscure demands of the situation, you end up in the bird barracks, training seagulls to shit on the periscopes of enemy submarines. But you didn't come here to listen to me complain about my station in the service. No. You came to learn. I need not remind you that you'll require every bit of your knowledge out here. Simply to survive. Our position is hopeless. The enemy is everywhere. He has the material, the momentum, the cooperation of the natives, and time is on his side. We have only our brain power. Pay attention. Your life depends on it.

The reliability of incoming intelligence depends on two factors: the probable truth of the information itself, and the credibility of its source. Information that contradicts known facts has a low 'probability of truth' rating. Think of an example.

Information coming from a notoriously unreliable source has a very low probability rating. Think of an example.

Or from a source that could not conceivably have come into possession of the information. Think of an example.

Now. Even with a mass of scrupulously assessed information—where there is an enemy whose moves you *must* anticipate, decision making is complex. The Basic Rule: The *more* likely an opponent's action *seems,* the *less* likely it *becomes*—as he will foresee that you will foresee it. He's clever. He'll change his plans—try to fool you. Therefore, the less likely an enemy's action becomes, the *more* likely it is that the enemy will resort to exactly that strategem. If it seems impossible—it's certain. Think of an example.

We are moving out at dawn to attack point B. I am presently sending out false information that we intend to attack point A. I am also giving out information that we will *attempt* to *convince* the enemy that we are going to attack point B. If the enemy should intercept any of our real communiqués in regard to our target B, rather than the false ones concerning A, they will think that those actually genuine pieces of information are only part of the attempt to deceive them.

I receive many intelligence reports on the enemy daily. I cross file them carefully in my Book of Intelligence. I attempt to assess their relevance and truth. However, I have not seen the enemy themselves for quite some time—years. But I understand their strategy in this. They wish to convince me that this is all some kind of game. Once this speculation has hold of my mind, and I relax my vigilance, they'll be on me like sewer rats, ripping at my throat. But, of course. . . .

6.

TRANSLATOR: You see. You torture your mind to find modern equivalents for what seems to be ancient wisdom, and you end up revealing the seemingly obscure and certainly repetitious conversations of military officers, or peasants, or hotel-keepers, fishermen, senile nuns at roadside shrines. It's indicative of the fate of serious scholarship in our time that, for the pittance Mr. Zendavesta pays me, I continue to struggle with this impossibly recalcitrant text.

However, there is one dim light. Structure. I'm fairly sure this book presupposes, as a frame device, the existence of a group of companions, who were originally ten in number. Whether these characters relate to actual people, or are pure inventions, I have no idea. The author seems obsessed with their moving from place to place like peripatetic shadows.

The Chinese setting itself is also subject to debate: I've come to believe it may well be a fiction. I'm almost certain that the book relies on geographical information about China plagiarized from a certain Child's Picture Atlas of the World . . . though at times the author seems to have either misread this source, or is deliberately inventing locations which never existed.

Yet this Book of the Yellow Ancestor remains somehow fascinating. I understate the case. I have been up all night with it for days. I think of nothing else. It has even crossed my mind that this text may be identical to one or more of the fabled "hidden" books: The Book of the Black Pilgrimage—or the Book of Brightness of Rabbi Isaac the Blind, or even—the legendary Epistle of Illusion and Caution.

It's even crossed my mind that Chinese may not be its original language . . . that this work in front of me is itself a translation, or a translation . . . of a translation . . . of a translation. . . .

7.

WAITRESS: Will that be all?
THIEF: What?
WAITRESS: You having dessert?
THIEF: Uh, yeah. Gimme some pie.
WAITRESS: Apple, cherry, lemon meringue? Key lime, rhubarb, pecan, peach, pumpkin? Boston cream?
ED: I quit.
WAITRESS: You're breaking my heart. Where you going?
ED: I'm southbound.

(*Ed is dragging what looks like the body of a man wrapped in brown paper and string. Ticket windows.*)

TICKET SELLER: What's the situation?
ED: Through the sharp hawthorn blows the cold wind.

TICKET SELLER: Too bad. What are you doing about it?
ED: Going south.
TICKET SELLER: How many?
ED: Party of one.
TICKET SELLER: If that thing's gonna ride, it needs a ticket.
ED: It'll fit on my lap.
TICKET SELLER: The hell it will. Pay or walk.

(*Ed checks his money. Not enough.*)

ED: They used to let John ride the hound for free. Travelled everywhere with him. But this is sweet goodbye. You people are in luck. Deep Sea Ed is caught short here, so I gotta unload my prize possession: the genuine preserved and mummified body of John Wilkes Booth, the most famous assassin of all time. I got the papers and everything. Affidavits from doctors. Got 'em framed—some of 'em. I got an x-ray photo of the fractured leg where he hit the stage floor. Even got a ring. You can mention that he swallowed it while attempting to disguise himself as he ran. You found it in the mummy's stomach. Even got a B on it. Get it? B for Booth.

   Look, you can make it over Egyptian if you want. Rig it with a battery so it wiggles. Jesus. You people don't know what you're looking at. This attraction took in five hundred dollars a day last season. You do that good with what you're showing? John Wilkes here makes money when everything else on the lot is dead. I built the fucker, and I'd a run him all winter in a goddamn storefront if I didn't have to go back to Canada. My mother's in a fucking clinic in fucking Winnipeg, and you people are hassling me.

   Look, I don't know what kind of trade you got, but if it ain't fun and fulfilling, try the show business. Hey, I'm begging you. Take him off my hands. All right. I made my offer, you turned me down. I ain't saying you won't regret it, 'cause you will. (*To the Ticket Seller.*) Gimme one.
TICKET SELLER: Winnipeg?
ED: Hell, no. Look, can I leave something in the baggage claim. I'll be back to pick it up in a few days. . . .
WAITRESS: Will that be all?
THIEF: What else you got?
WAITRESS: Jello. (*Music.*)
THIEF: I'll have some of that jello.
WAITRESS: Red? Or green? Red? Or green?
THIEF: I was telling you, I'm running away, cause I went over my head, you know. I mean I grabbed something good, real good—and I don't know what to do with it. It's the kind of thing—you had it and somebody took it——you'd kill people to get it back. See, I had a ring I found somewhere, so

I'm looking to sell it, and I hear about a guy in an office building . . . I'm in this corridor, see . . . wandering around, somebody's playing a radio behind one of these doors. . . .

8.

JEWELLER: I am a dealer in precious stones. This particular favorite of mine first turned up in India in 1712. Supposedly, the raw stone was ripped from the forehead of an Indian idol, and came into the hands of a trader from Sumatra, who was promptly torn to pieces by a pack of rabid dogs. But that, of course, is hearsay.

Louis XIV is said to have given it to the lovely Mme. Montespan as a mark of royal favor, which she lost soon afterwards. She became a nun at a Spanish convent, where she is rumored to have been badly mistreated by the sisters . . . It appeared again in London in 1847 as the stickpin of Prince Ivan Kanitovsky, who was murdered by a bellboy at the Connaught Hotel. Abdul Hamid of Turkey possessed it briefly until he was dethroned, and it was sold to Simon Montharides, whose carriage was dragged over a cliff by shying horses near the Borgo Pass, killing him, his wife, and two children. What a coincidence.

The stone was then placed by his executors in the Green Vaults of Dresden, which will be mentioned more than once this evening. The American actress who purchased it in 1930 was burned to death in the tragic fire at the Bijou theatre in Los Angeles. I bought it from her attorneys in 1971.

When I came into possession, the stone had its original Indian design. An idiotic waste. This first cutting and faceting had been done in Venice by Joseph Asscher. The months of tension preceding his botch of the job caused him to be hospitalized for a nervous disability . . . a small sanitarium near the Grand Canal. Still there, I believe. . . .

The decision of how to cleave and cut the stone so as to reveal its full power was the most difficult of my life. I considered the English Mazarin, the star cut, devised by the Parisian master, Caire. My final decision was the right one. The stone is now a triple cut brilliant, with one hundred and one facets around its table. I did this.

I have possessed the stone for ten years now. I spend each night alone with it.

THIEF: So I'm in this corridor, see, wandering around this office building. I know the guy's name, but I don't remember the office number. I try one.

JEWELLER: Yes?

THIEF: Mr. Ravensburg?

JEWELLER: Yes, I am Ravensburg.

THIEF: I'm here to sell something. A ring. It's a family heirloom.

JEWELLER: I buy nothing.

THIEF: But I was told you could help me out.

JEWELLER: I do not buy anything.
THIEF: You don't buy anything *tonight?*
JEWELLER: Not tonight, not ever.
THIEF: It's my mother's wedding ring. This guy Bernard, he sent me. You know Bernard?
JEWELLER: I do not have the honor.
THIEF: Then I guess there's a mistake here. I'm looking for Mr. Ravensburg.
JEWELLER: I am Mr. Ravensburg.
THIEF: But you don't buy anything.
JEWELLER: No. Here we do cutting and shaping.
THIEF: Hey, maybe there's someone else in this building named Ravensburg.
JEWELLER: No doubt. In this building, it's a very common name.

(*Jeweller turns away, Thief grabs him from behind. Music of distant motel. A "No Vacancy" sign.*)

9.

DEEP SEA EDNA: You know how to read? Words?
THIEF: I can read—but there's nothing else for miles, and I thought I'd ask you personally . . .

(*Edna looks him over, changes sign.*)

EDNA: I got one room I always leave empty. Room ten. The last guy I put in there—pool hustler from Grand Forks, North Dakota—died in his sleep. He died of a dream.
THIEF: Well, that's too bad, but I'll lie down anywhere. Besides, I didn't know him. His ghost won't trouble me.
EDNA: Good enough. (*Hands key.*) You woke me up, so tell me some lies. What are you doing here?
THIEF: Well . . . there's a man in town that won't be happy till he sells me a dog. I gotta see him.
EDNA: Good.
THIEF: Thanks. Uh, I don't like to bother you, but you got something to eat? A sandwich and a beer or something . . . I can pay you . . .
EDNA: Sorry. Usta have a coffee shop. "24 hours. We never close." My husband ran it. Cook, and a good one too. But every time he gets twenty bucks in his pocket he thinks it's time to see the world. Bastard's been gone for six months this time. He'll come back—but I don't suggest you wait up for him. Everything's in the room—towels, magazines. And if you get lonely, don't ring my bell.

(*Edna is gone.*)

THIEF (STUDENT, GIRL, AUTHOR): This magazine is called *Voyeur*. Uh . . . it's full of color photos of girls. They look like they're enjoying themselves. Nothing to read though—Ah . . . Here's a page with words on it. Letters to *Voyeur*. Hmmn. Dear *Voyeur*: I'm a freshman at a midwestern college. I was cruising the motel strip one night after a few beers, when I see this blonde chick with her thumb out, wearing a pair of the tightest cut offs I'd ever seen. My bonger jumped in my levis as I pulled up and asked where she was going. "With you," she said. When the speedometer hit 70, she reached over and began to rub me through my jeans. I couldn't believe my luck. I thought I was gonna explode. We pulled into the nearest motel. As soon as we got in the room her tongue was down my throat, but then she pulled away. She said she needed some champagne to really get her in the mood.

I remembered a liquor store a few miles back, so I lit out for the car. As I pulled away, I could see her through the drawn shade, taking off her clothes.

I bought a couple of bottles of California Brut and headed back up the strip. Then I realized—I didn't remember which motel we'd checked into. They flashed by one after the other: Northwood Inn, Hotel Seagull, Lazy Man Motel, Sombrero Inn, Flamingo, Travellers Inn, Blue Dolphin, Iroquois Motel. I turned around, drove back the other way, hoping something would jog my beer soaked brain. My dick was dying. Finally, I saw one I thought might be it . . . the Blue Spruce. I pulled in, and then I realized—I forgot the room number. The place was quiet as death. I took a guess, knocked on a door. A fat man in a t-shirt opened it. Behind him I could see a woman lying on a bed, reading a magazine. As a matter of fact, it was *Voyeur*. He said, "What the hell do you want?" "To give you this champagne," I said. I handed it to him, drove back to the dorm, and went to sleep. I keep thinking about that girl, wondering if she's still there waiting for me. Sincerely, a Student.

(By the end of this speech the Thief is seated alongside Edna—two lawn chairs, a birdbath.)

EDNA: Fascinating. Listen, I know you're running. Why don't you run with me. I got a little sideline I take out on the road. Deep Sea Edna's Shooting Gallery and Marine Museum. You'll do for setup and takedown. You can feed the fish.
THIEF: Well, I might be better off on my own. I could bring trouble.
EDNA: Trouble's a friend of mine. Stay in your tracks, whoever's looking for you'll find you sure. Probably stab you in your sleep behind a billboard. Go down my road for a while, you'll disappear. Besides, you can help me look around.

THIEF: For what?

EDNA: For Ed.

THIEF: But I don't know anything about fish.

EDNA: Don't worry. I have an eye for talent. And if people are looking for you, get a disguise . . pair of glasses or something. We leave in the morning. Southbound. (*Edna exits.*)

THIEF: But I want you people to understand that running scared isn't my full-time occupation. I mean, your mind keeps working too. I'm a writer. I write Margo postcards. And I read—magazines. You can read a lot of interesting things in magazines. This one here is the *UFO Review,* published by Sublime Publications, and it's got articles like "I Was Transported to Venus," and "PLATILLO VOLADOR . . . Saucer Over Brazil." But in case you think I'm only interested in the sensational—there's another article in here that's different. I been thinking about it—reading it over and over. It's by a Mrs. Carl Lammle, who is someone I'd like to talk to sometime. It's called:

ALL: "The WORLD OF COINCIDENCE."

10.

MRS. LAMMLE: All of you are, I'm sure, familiar with what I term the WORLD OF COINCIDENCE. In this world, events seem to be more connected . . . than they are in our everyday world, where they most often seem, random, absurd—if not perniciously unrelated to each other. In the world of coincidence, however, the most common expression is:

ALL: What a coincidence!

MRS. LAMMLE: For example:

MAN: Excuse me, sweetheart, you dropped your fish . . . I mean . . . scarf.

WOMAN: Thanks, mister . . . (*To herself.*) . . . Odd he should say that. Last night I dreamed of a fish.

MRS. LAMMLE: Or . . .

MAN: Excuse me, sweetheart, you dropped your scarf . . . I mean . . . fish.

WOMAN: Thanks, mister. Odd he should say that. Last night I dreamed of a scarf.

MRS. LAMMLE: Of course.

OTHER MAN NO. 1: I was in the middle of writing my chapter on wind-force, when a sudden breeze blew all my papers all over the room.

OTHER MAN NO. 2: Remarkable. (*To himself.*) Odd that he should say that. Last night I dreamed of papers, blowing all around me . . .

MRS. LAMMLE: Yes. Our common idea of cause and effect is succinctly illustrated in the common expression: "Just one thing after another." This notion is linked to our childish ideas of the nature of space and time. In the World of Coincidence, these ideas are null, and void. In man's original mind, as we find it among primitive peoples, space and time have a very precarious existence. They become fixed concepts only in the course of our mental development. Actually, the truth is, that in themselves, space and time consist of *nothing*. They are only concepts born of the discriminating activity of the conscious mind. They do, however, form the indispensable coordinates for describing bodies in motion. Think of an example. A ball rolling down an incline, a man traveling south along a certain highway . . . Let's get on with it, shall we. I have been keeping a personal journal of coincidence for thirty years. After a very fruitful year or two, the question arises forcefully in the seeking mind . . . Was I simply more aware of coincidences by keeping this journal—or was I . . . making them . . . happen? Green Hill? Ed Green, Fred Berry and Ted Hill. FACT. John McCabe of Fulham Road in the Bronx, New York was listening to a record of "Cry of the Wild Goose" by Frankie Laine . . .

SONG: I must go where the wild goose goes, I must fly where the wild goose flies . . .

MRS. LAMMLE: . . . when a Canadian goose crashed through his bedroom window. FACT.

As the Danforth family of Peru, Indiana were watching the sinking of the Titanic on a TV movie of the week, just as the iceberg hits the ship, a large block of ice falls through the roof of their ranch style home, smashes the TV to smithereens. FACT.

Alphonso Bedoya was crossing Prince's Canal in Amsterdam. He was struck and killed by a green taxi carrying a passenger named Ravensburg. His brother, Armando Bedoya, was also killed in Amsterdam, while crossing Prince's Canal, by a green taxi—carrying a passenger named Ravensburg—ten years later. FACT.

At times an expert witness has coincidentally been present at the scene of the coincidental . . . as when Dr. A.D. Bajkov, the noted ichthyologist, visiting the United States, was bombarded with fish from the sky, shortly after breakfast in Biloxi, Mississippi. FACT.

But let's take a more ordinary example. Let's say you decide to go to the oculist to get a pair of glasses. You walk into the shop, past the displays of glasses and frames in the window. A bell rings. Once inside, you notice that the oculist's shop seems also to be an outlet for the books of a company called Sublime Publications. . . .

11.

TRANSLATOR: Introducing Mr. Zendavesta, my employer in this suspect venture. He should have just finished his usual breakfast: quail eggs in which the blebs of fertilization are kept raw, lace cake, jompoo juice, and jello. As the fisherman can infer the presence of the great whale from a single bubble on the sea—so Mr. Zendavesta claims to be able to discern the . . .

ZENDAVESTA: The Book of the Yellow Ancestor! The translation! You've finished!

TRANSLATOR: Are you joking?

ZENDAVESTA: The wisdom of the Yellow Ancestor is no joking matter. You're almost finished?

TRANSLATOR: I've made some headway. But this text still seems extremely unreliable.

ZENDAVESTA: Unreliable to you—perhaps a rock of sanity to me. Forge ahead. Translate! What have you got so far?

TRANSLATOR: Well, there are some completed sections, but they're really . . . odd.

ZENDAVESTA: My ears are yours.

TRANSLATOR: O.K. . . . I'm fairly sure about this one—"The Genie's Pharmacy—prescription ten. Feed a small duckling on rose petals, mixed with oil and blood. When the bird is grown and its feathers come out red, kill it, dry it, crush it, feathers and all, and take a teaspoon of this powder every day for three hundred days."

ZENDAVESTA: That's it?

TRANSLATOR: That section, yeah.

ZENDAVESTA: And for what condition is this the cure?

TRANSLATOR: It doesn't say.

ZENDAVESTA: Of course.

TRANSLATOR: I might be mistaken about the characters for prescription. Perhaps "document" or "dispatch" . . . I also had trouble with . . .

ZENDAVESTA: Please. Sublime Publications owes you a debt it can never repay. Your photo on the jacket? A certainty. Tell me, are there any passages that seem to be *directions* to a place?

TRANSLATOR: Not yet.

ZENDAVESTA: Keep at it. Don't fail me. I'm leaving shortly for the Oculists' Convention near Mexico City. I'm sure you'll be kind enough to meet me there. We'll work together by the pool. A change of scene might calm your fevered brain. Your ticket. (*Bell.*)

THIEF: Anybody here?

ZENDAVESTA: (*To Translator.*) Excuse me. A customer. Wait here. Browse. (*To Thief.*) Yes?

THIEF: I want to get a pair of clear glasses with just glass in them, you know.

ZENDAVESTA: I know. Read the top line please.

THIEF: I can't make any sense of that.

ZENDAVESTA: Fine. Lie down. This will only take a moment. (*Zendavesta examines the Thief.*)

TRANSLATOR: Zendavesta used to be an optical lens grinder in Chicago. He lived in a small room at the Diamond Hotel. He was a bachelor. He thought a lot about the nature of this life we lead, and his own particular destiny. He often lay awake nights, turning these two questions over in his mind like dice in a cage.

One day he was walking down West Madison Street after work, when he saw a man wearing a sandwich board sign, which read: WE LIVE INSIDE. The man was selling a pamphlet for ten cents, also titled WE LIVE INSIDE. The lens-grinder bought a copy. It changed his entire life. Years later he could be heard to remark:

ZENDAVESTA: I read it in bed, and before I fell asleep that night, I *was* inside.

THIEF: What'd you say?

ZENDAVESTA: (*To Thief.*) Ah! Just as I suspected. The green quinsy. Invariably leads to blindness and insanity. This condition requires an immediate surgical procedure.

THIEF: Hey, look. I just . . .

ZENDAVESTA: Stop. I can anticipate your query. The answer is: would I tell you you needed an operation if you didn't?

THIEF: I'll take my chances. Gimme the glasses and I'll get out of here.

ZENDAVESTA: Perhaps you'd like to purchase a new face, something so attractive that social graces will become unnecessary? You'll be able to get away with it, if you follow me . . .

THIEF: No thanks. I'll be going now.

ZENDAVESTA: Just a moment. You seem like a malleable young man, who's in trouble. I'm preparing an expedition, and am currently attempting to hire a muscular assistant who's not bright enough to cause any harm.

I have sent every senator and representative in the Congress of our United States a registered letter, on the letterhead of Sublime Publications, appealing for immediate financing to equip us for *the adventure*. Knowing their childish prejudices, I enclosed my certificate of sanity with each appeal. The results are only just beginning to flow into my offices. As soon as these funds arrive, we depart.

I'll take you where jewellers and policemen will never find you. We'll even send for Margo.

THIEF: Margo? How do you know . . .

ZENDAVESTA: Where are we going, you ask? Young man, the new cosmogony has been revealed to me. The key is simple. We live inside the earth. Modern astronomers are perfectly correct, except that they have everything inside out. The entire cosmos is like an egg. We live on the inner surface of a hollow shell, and inside the hollow are the sun, the moon, the stars, the planets, and the comets in their courses. What, you ask, is outside the shell? Nothing. Absolutely nothing. The inside is all there is.

However, at a certain point in the shell, there is a hole. A tiny hole, through which a man could enter that endless effluvium of endless absence, to annihilate himself in bliss. I'm talking to you about the resurrection, with a difference.

Dark Ride 75

THIEF: Yeah . . .
ZENDAVESTA: As soon as the exact location of this hole is revealed, the funds assembled—we set out! We have, of course, been subjected to insolent ridicule in our attempts to bring this knowledge before the public.
THIEF: You ever think about UFO's?
ZENDAVESTA: The things you call unidentified flying objects are neither objects, nor flying, nor unidentified. We know very well who they are.

(*Bell.*)

ZENDAVESTA: Wait here. Browse.
THIEF: (*To Translator.*) You . . read these books?
TRANSLATOR: Some of them.
THIEF: They interesting?
TRANSLATOR: Some of them.
THIEF: Tell him I couldn't stay, hah. And good luck with your expedition.
TRANSLATOR: I doubt I'll be going . . . Hey! What's your name?

(*The Thief is gone.*)

ZENDAVESTA: (*To Mrs. Lammle.*) Yes?
MRS. LAMMLE: I'm not interested in your philosophy. I want to pick up a pair of glasses.
ZENDAVESTA: Name?
MRS. LAMMLE: Mrs. Carl Lammle.
ZENDAVESTA: Yes. Of course. Walk this way . . .
TRANSLATOR: Mr. Zendavesta claims to have the world's most complete library of the occult, excepting only the collection stored in the Green Vaults of Dresden. Maybe there's a manuscript copy of the Book of Brightness, or the *Epistle of Illusion and Caution* . . . Hmmn . . . *Nine Holes of Jade* by Soo Ling, *The Candid Memoirs of a Hong Kong Call Girl. Ribald Russian Classics, The Wit and Wisdom of Uninhibited Peasants* . . . an issue of *Voyeur* . . . Here's one called *Venus in India* by a Captain Ernest Devereaux, *The Amorous Adventures of a Gallant Soldier.* . . .

This one's got an odd frontispiece . . . Looks like an engraving of a long corridor, anonymous office building. One door is partly open, and I can see a small room within. A man sits at a table, a safe behind him, diamond dust and oil coat his fingers. . . .

12.

JEWELLER: I am the dealer in precious stones. I know them, their sounds, their crystal hums.

GENERAL: (*Writing.*) Crystal hums . . .

JEWELLER: I am a patient man. I studied in Amsterdam for ten years to learn to mark the stones for the chisel. Ten more years to cleave. Place the chisel, kiss it, and the stone falls into its parts. Like men. One tap, and into parts invisible. Now the stone I love has been stolen from me, and I will have it back, and I will wash it clean in the thief's blood.

I'll explain myself, if you don't mind. I met a girl once. She was a Dutch girl, and she worked in a bookstore in Amsterdam, on Prince's Canal. Children's books. She also played the flute in an amateur orchestra. I came to buy a book in English for my brother's son in America. For his birthday. She helped me choose. I chose one about a monkey.

GENERAL: (*Writing.*) . . . monkey . . .

JEWELLER: I stared at her the whole time. She was not embarrassed. We had coffee.

She loved me. When I tell it to you now it is difficult, even for me who lived it, to believe. For one year, she brought me into the world. We went to cafés, the theatre, even to the countryside. At home, she would watch as I marked the stones. She was quiet, and asked for nothing. I thought I was reborn under a new sun.

One night she met the conductor of the state symphony at a party at the university. One week later she went to live with him in a house in a suburb of Amsterdam. For a month, I could not believe this simple truth. Her smell was everywhere.

After she moved away, I cut the stone. It had arrived a year ago, and I had spent months delaying, staring at it as she watched me. I always felt that my mark was wrong, and if I cut—the stone would fall into worthless fragments. That night, I opened the Zohar to the Book of Brightness, and though I read it without understanding, it calmed me. I erased my mark. And then I bled from my nose and mouth, and the blood flowed down onto the stone, a transluscent coat of my blood, and the stone shone clearer than ever. I remember the open Zohar, the blood, the light, the diamond dust from the polisher, the view out over the canals, the passing boats of the tourists. Then, almost without my noticing—the tap of the hammer on the blade.

It has been said that God had compassion on Adam after he banished him from Eden, and sent the archangel Raziel to give him a book that could guide him back to Paradise, if he could learn to read it. The exact form of this "Book of Raziel" is unknown. I once thought of it as the entire creation. Now I know that it exists, condensed within one diamond eye—in a thief's pocket.

Once I spent my nights looking into the facets of the stone to see the past, the future, and the roads between. Now I can only look into my mind's picture of it. The blue glow fills my skull. I can't find the thief, but I see something he'll follow as I follow the stone. Do you see it, General? See it.

GENERAL: *(Aside.)* This private work can be distressing to a professional soldier. *(To Jeweller.)* Right, sir. Just give me the information. We'll screw the enemy to the wall.

JEWELLER: Into the tenth facet! An apartment in this city! She's dreaming, and she thinks my eye is something in her dream. She wakes, opens a novel . . . Odd book, must read it sometime. She closes the book. She turns on the TV. Perfect. General, get your hat and stick. We have work to do.

13.

MARGO: My Sony is a one-way communication system, sending me words and pictures that never end. They're always changing, and despite this, I always understand them. My TV can communicate with me, if I'm awake, and watching. To communicate with me means to say stuff, or show me stuff I understand. If you say something to me I don't understand, we're not communicating, are we? If I say something to you and you don't understand, we're not communicating. Are we? But we're communicating right now.

If we keep communicating like this—so we understand each other—it'll only lead to little ripples in our context, this world of common words and pictures that allows us to communicate in the first place. Like me and my TV—it never does much more than give a little shuffle to the cards I've already got. It's pleasant, but now I'm turning it off. I need a new deck.

JEWELLER: General, do something. I'm not interested in her philosophy.

GENERAL: Why don't you forget everything you know about all that and let us get on with it.

MARGO: If you step out of this pleasant sensation of understanding, and the world that makes it possible, you stop communicating. These postcards from my lover are perfect: Notes from somewhere else torn up and delivered by the wind.

GENERAL: Why don't you forget everything you know about all that and let us get on with it . . .

MARGO: I miss the crazy bastard. I did book—I did TV—now record player.

(Music.)

GENERAL AND JEWELLER: Gotcha.

(Margo screams.)

ACT II

14.

Mrs. Lammle, Margo, Deep Sea Edna.

MRS. LAMMLE: Yes. Our Bible is a deep mine of treasure for the student of coincidence. The Book of Revelation lists ten plagues, ten seals, and ten archangels: Michael, Gabriel, Zakiel, Uriel, Jamalel, Nuriel, Samael, Fleuriel, Ariel and last, but not least, Raziel. And how many heads has Babylon, the mother of harlots? Ten. FACT.

One particular jewel in this mine is the story of Jonah. The prophet's dark ride in the belly of the whale—three days. Christ's tenure in the tomb before his resurrection—three days. FACT.

And now, from my journal. Twenty years ago, when she was four years old, a young woman, who shall remain anonymous, stood quietly outside a gypsy fortune telling parlor in Chicago, while her mother had her palm read. The Gypsy, a certain Madame Edna, . . . Marcel, would you bring out the model, please? Thank you, Marcel. The Gypsy, a certain Madame Edna, gave the girl a Charlotte Russe, insisting that she try it.

EDNA: Try it.

MRS. LAMMLE: She loved it. Recently, while travelling far from home, the girl saw her second Charlotte Russe, in the window of an expensive restaurant. When she entered and ordered it, she found that the Charlotte Russe was reserved for a special customer. Imagine her surprise when this customer turned out to be Madame Edna, looking exactly the same after all these years. They shared the Charlotte Russe, and both seemed astonished at meeting once again over the same confection.

At some time in the future, this young woman attends a formal banquet near Mexico City. To her surprise it features Charlotte Russes as dessert. She naturally tells her companions about her curious encounters with Madame Edna. Meanwhile, Madame Edna herself has been invited to another, rather less formal affair, in the basement of the same hotel. She loses her way in the maze of the building's corridors, knocks on a door to ask for directions. Our young woman, holding a Charlotte Russe in her hand, opens it. They stare at each other. What a coincidence.

I still tell these stories, but I'm no longer sure what they signify. Perhaps I'm tired. I want to get away for a while—from Carl—that's my husband—and my life here. Lately, I've been dreaming of trains—little locomotives, with pleasant curls of smoke twirling into blue skies, crossing little child's maps of the continent, heading south to some resting place under a new sun. I need a vacation.

15.

GENERAL: Hmmm. A dispatch from the front. Thank you, Marcel. Perhaps a nice promotion. Recognition of my efforts at our particularly exposed station is long overdue.

However, it's possible that the news enclosed will take a grimmer turn. Battle statistics. The valor of my second in command has long been suspect . . . The truth is that I left the station in charge of my waterboy, whose command of English is far from . . . But why speculate? The applicable rule in these complex situations: never assume you know where you're going, till you've gotten there. In other words, you've got to suck it and see. *(Opens envelope.)*

Hmmm. It seems that in my absence our position has been overrun by the enemy, the remainder of our unit, destroyed, and my personal possessions burnt to ashes. I have been reassigned to the bird barracks. "Report immediately."

I refuse. As you've seen, I am already embarked on a new career. I am a kidnapper. However, this is not as tawdry as it sounds. Margo actually behaves as if we're taking her on holiday. In any case, as Mussolini said to the British ambassador when their limousine ran over a child in the streets of Naples . . . "Never look back."

This adventure will also serve as a snazzy final fillip to my memoirs. Memoirs with a difference. Not only my actual experience in the service, but my dreams, fantasies—the inner man. And I have developed a compositional technique. Among all the methods of writing, I may not be certain my own way is the best, but I am absolutely sure it is the most religious. I begin by writing the first sentence, and trust to almighty God for the second.

But let's be frank for a moment. This jeweller is a madman. When he returned from this private clinic in the mountains, his imagination was diseased. However, he's paying me. His plan? Now that we've kidnapped the girl, we follow the postcards she receives from this thief to track him down. Then we use her as bait to draw him into our figurative maw. We get train tickets . . .

We head south . . .

We cross over the border into Mexico.

We race through the desert, its stark beauty interrupted by an occasional panorama of local business: Panchito's Tacos, Valdez Auto-Repair. The jeweller is abstracted. Margo is resigned . . . or pleased. She knows we're taking her to him. She cannot imagine what this jeweller plans to do to her lover, once we find him.

CONDUCTOR: Tickets? Tickets?

JEWELLER: Why don't you ask the engineers in the locomotive for their tickets?

CONDUCTOR: Because they're driving the train.

JEWELLER: So are we.

MARGO: Right.

JEWELLER: She's a quick study.

GENERAL: I examine the final postcard for clues. Seems to be a souvenir card from some seedy roadside attraction. The thief must be gone from there. Postmark is ten days old . . . We rush on toward the posh hotel outside Mexico City, where the Jeweller has engaged a number of ballrooms to bait our trap.

MARGO: So this is Mexico.

JEWELLER: Yes.

MARGO: It's just what I thought it would be. I've seen it on TV . . . dead cows.

JEWELLER: Do you love me?

MARGO: Love you? You're kidnapping me. Besides, I don't even know you. I mean maybe if I knew you for years or something . . . I doubt it. No.

JEWELLER: You may change your mind. You may discover that love is not so much a feeling . . . as it is a situation.

GENERAL: Though this thief seems both dangerous and resourceful, my jeweller is confident he'll rise to the bait, like a great whale coming up from the bottom of the sea.

JEWELLER: Confident? No. Certain. I had the stone, and it brought me the evil fate to lose it. Now I pursue, but he has the stone, and the weight of its power slows him, his legs grow heavy, his alertness dwindles, and we have him! Only a man of learning and restraint can possess the stone without it leading him to his doom.

GENERAL: Right. Hmmm. The picture on this latest postcard is curious. It shows a woman in a polka dot housedress standing in front of what looks like a torn curtain with a few holes in it. She has an idiot grin on her face, and over her head is a badly lettered sign, that clearly once said DEEP SEA ED'S World of Wonders, but two new letters—NA, have been squeezed in after ED , . .

16.

EDNA: You curious about love?
THIEF: Yeah.
EDNA: Psst. Here's the secret. It's a mystery. One of 'em. The truth is that loving Ed is just something I do, you know. I don't think about it anymore. He was the original owner of this popgun palace and marine museum. When I met him he specialized in window sleeps, went into trances in store windows to advertise furniture sales. "Suspended animation. Hasn't eaten for two weeks!" He was doing it at Watson Discount. After Mom was asleep, one, two in the morning—I'd go down there and slip food to him, bags fulla greasy tacos, sneaking down Main Street like a thief. I was seventeen . . . When he left town, I left with him.

You still don't know what the hell to do, do you?
THIEF: Well, I'm still trying to hide . . .
EDNA: Get a straight job. That'll hide you. Nobody looks at working people. My brother's got a body shop in Las Cruces. That's on the border. Means the crosses.
THIEF: I don't know anything about the insides of cars. I don't really know how to do anything.
EDNA: Then go into show business. Take that girl along. She could do the parachuting, which is easy for women and they enjoy it too. Gives 'em a thrill. I used to do it with Ed. Last time was a state fair in Jackson, Mississippi. I lost myself up there, landed in an empty gondola heading east. I stopped jumping after that, and Ed was scared, so we got a Mexican kid named Eduardo. Lot of style. Made himself up in a batman suit. He did one season with us. Next year some circus picked him up. Took him to Europe. His luck didn't hold. He was doing his batman jump in Venice when his shrouds tangled and that was it. Never had a chance. Batman into the Grand Canal.

For a while, me and Ed were big time. Owned a carnival on the Canadian circuit, even did the Alberta Provincial Fair. Had a Hall of History, all kinds of figures in dramatic tableaux. Looked realer than hell. Ed made them all himself. Paper mache and spit.

And then Ed got religion. He invented a new ride for the midway, his idea being that its motion would provide a spiritual experience for the clientele. It was called the Ezekial, and that's what it looked like: wheel in a wheel, way in the middle of the air. The little wheel run by faith, and the big wheel run by the grace of God . . . Well, on its first run with live customers some drunk teenager flies out of the damn thing. Ed is sued by these lawyers, and he loses everything—his carnival, the Ezekial ride, everything. Then he disappeared. When I found him again he was a fry cook at a place called the Embers.

ED: Here's your two over light, I got a burger royale working . . .

EDNA: It was back then that we started doing the casket of death. Ten sticks of dynamite, lead shielding, some cotton in your ears, a bag of stage blood, and they faint in the seats. When we were testing—I learned something. Best thing I can teach you. We'd light the fuse and walk away. It'd burn down in about five minutes, but sometimes it seemed like an hour waiting for the charge to go off. That's what kills people. Time seems stretched. They figure the fuse has gone out, they go back to check, and are right on top of it when she blows. I learned to give it plenty of time . . .

MAN: I'm not interested in philosophy. We want to see the fish. One, please.

EDNA: Hey Mister. If she's old enough to enjoy the show, she's old enough to need a ticket. Take 'em in.

(*The Thief is gone with the customers.*)

ZENDAVESTA: Are you showing people to these fish, or vice-versa?

EDNA: Cute. Think it over. You're the one who paid at the door.

ZENDAVESTA: Yes, indeed. Should I be amused, or is this somehow educational?

EDNA: Educational. These fish are quiet, and besides, they know the secrets of the deep.

ZENDAVESTA: Do you mind if I sit down a moment, the better to contemplate these marvels?

EDNA: Help yourself.

ZENDAVESTA: I am Mr. Zendavesta, a humble explorer of the etheric borderlands. I'd appreciate it if you'd examine this small pamphlet, entitled WE LIVE INSIDE. You might find it instructive.

EDNA: Tell me if I have this right. You are a harmless crank.

ZENDAVESTA: Crank? Madame, I deplore cranks. The discoverer of the corpuscular theory of sounds, of kinematic relativity, of the cosmic donut, where are they now? Already dead, and buried alongside the Mad Hatter. I am a scientist.

EDNA: I'm proud of you. But I'm closing up now.

ZENDAVESTA: Please. I know what you think.

EDNA: Do you now?

ZENDAVESTA: Of course. There are two sides to every argument, and both of them are mine. You see, I was once a common voluptuary like yourself. Yet I soon realized that the ordinary mines of enjoyment are easily exhausted. I perceived that these crowded paths of pleasure turned back on themselves in diminishing spirals of decreasing delight. Once I had escaped the toils of the serpent of desire, my mind opened. Ideas descended on me like a flight of vultures on a dying antelope.

You're quite a handsome woman, you know. I've been looking for a group of brave companions to set out on a certain expedition I have in mind . . .

EDNA: Sorry. I gotta baby-sit that night.

ZENDAVESTA: Then perhaps something less total in its implications. I am also the entertainment coordinator at the upcoming World Oculists' convention at the extraordinary Hacienda Ramon on the outskirts of Mexico City. Perhaps you'd consent, for a fee, of course, to display these fish in some suitable. . . .

17.

JEWELLER: Margo—you are now the hostess for the annual World Oculists' Convention near Mexico City. We've published your photograph in all the newspapers.

GENERAL: Congratulations.

MARGO: Thank you.

JEWELLER: As usual, the oculists' affair is held at the legendary Hacienda Ramon. Your friend is in the neighborhood. He'll see your photo. He will come. He won't leave the stone behind, and I'll hear it singing in his pocket. It belongs in my forehead, a dim glow in the darkness of the temple, the incense spirals upward . . . Pardon my enthusiasm. Hmmm. It seems my new associate is late—or perhaps . . .

TRANSLATOR: Café con leche, por favor.

WAITRESS: Got it. Anything else?

TRANSLATOR: Yes. Some jello, please.

WAITRESS: Red? Or green?

JEWELLER: (*To Translator.*) Are you the taxidermist?

TRANSLATOR: No . . . I'm the translator.

JEWELLER: Who?

TRANSLATOR: I mean, no. I just stopped in for a drink on my way to . . .

JEWELLER: Thank you. Margo, you look lovely in this light. You remind me of someone . . .

MARGO: Really? How interesting.

JEWELLER: Do you play the flute?

MARGO: No.

JEWELLER: You could learn.

MARGO: Can I get another coco-loco?

JEWELLER: Of course . . . You know, I'd planned to immure you forever,

along with your clever boyfriend, in the Green Vaults of Dresden. I even brought my trowel along. But I've had a better idea.
GENERAL: Oh God. I hestiate to present you raw recruits with my informed speculation as to the nature of this jeweller's revenge. However, familiar as I am with illegal conduct in the line of duty, I have begun to prepare my alibi. "I don't know anything about all that, your honor. I was in Milwaukee at the time. At my brother's wedding. I danced with the bride. She was pregnant, only eighteen, a senior at St. Ann's. We danced till dawn."
TRANSLATOR: " 'When the fog is heavy on the road to the Emperor's Jewelled Garden, you hear voices all around you, shouting directions. Go south. When the fog burns away, no sign of travelers — no horses, no carriages, no tracks in the dust.' The man in bandages stopped talking, stood up slowly, and walked over to the window . . ."
WAITRESS: Anything else?
TRANSLATOR: Uh . . . say Miss . . . I'm a stranger here, and I thought you might . . . have a drink with me after work.
WAITRESS: I'd love to, cowboy, but we never close.
TRANSLATOR: What? But you can't mean that you . . .
WAITRESS: Will that be all?
GENERAL: (*To Margo.*) You're thinking about him, aren't you?
MARGO: I think about him all the time.
GENERAL: I was married once. I loved my wife. Loved the children.

One day, after we'd been married for ten years, when I came home from work my wife kissed me with surprising passion. She'd bought me a present—some kind of aftershave. In bed that night she was heaven. She did everything I like best, and that woman knew me. I fell asleep full of renewed hope for our future.

The next morning before I left for work, she wrapped her arms around me, as if she never wanted me to go. Finally I got to the garage, got in my car, turned the key in the ignition, and the world exploded. She'd had her boyfriend wire a bomb behind the dashboard. I almost died. I had so much glass in my face it took the doctors two weeks to get it out of me.
MARGO: Why are you telling me this?
GENERAL: So you'll understand.
MARGO: Understand what?
WAITRESS: What'll it be, folks?

(*Deep Sea Ed comes out of the kitchen, goes to the Translator's table.*)

ED: Hello, slick. Got a cigarette?
TRANSLATOR: Sorry. I don't smoke.
ED: You new in town?
TRANSLATOR: Well, I . . .

WAITRESS: A Blue Plate Special, heavy on the gravy, Enchilada combination, and a coco-loco.
ED: I quit.
WAITRESS: Don't tell me. Tell your mother. Tell those nice folks at table ten.
ED: The hell with them. I gotta get my ticket.

(*Ticket Windows.*)

TICKET SELLER: How many?
ED: I'm a first class grill man, a soldier of fortune, and a doctor of medicine. You happen to be looking at the inventor and sole distributor of Deep Sea Ed's analgesic balm, an unfailing cure for mumps, measles, malaria and all other diseases beginning with the letter M.

I am also an artiste—sole inspiration and executor of Deep Sea Ed's Hall of History, a faithful and three dimensional panorama, a solemn reminder of the grandeur of bygone days, including a diorama of the glacial age of the cave man, constructed under the supervision of college professors; a tableau of the hideous murder of Prince Kanitovsky by a bellboy at the Connaught Hotel; a complete model of Ford's theatre, featuring the great President Lincoln, and his vile assassin, John Wilkes Booth!

I made all these figures that you see before you, in poses taken from the life. Lessons to be learned! Not only entertaining, but educational as well!

Hell, that show is what you call defunct.

It's a moving world, my masters, and the sands are forever shifting.

The Central Labor Service down on Aveñida Juarez got me something near Mexico City. World tells you something, you go along.
TICKET SELLER: I'm not interested in philosophy. I'm interested in selling tickets. What's the situation?
ED: Through the sharp hawthorn blows the cold wind.
TICKET SELLER: Too bad. What are you doing about it?
ED: Going south.
TICKET SELLER: How many?
ED: One, please.

(*Margo to the Translator's table.*)

MARGO: Hi.
TRANSLATOR: Hi.
MARGO: You know, there's only really two ideas about the things people believe. One is—only the stuff *everyone* believes is true, like the sun is wonderful, and there's probably some kind of God inside, and hurting people isn't nice . . . that stuff. The alternate choice is: If everyone believes it, how *could* it be true? I mean, it's obvious that everyone else is crazy, that only

the stuff *I* believe is true. I mean, if anyone agrees with me about something, I start thinking my idea must be pretty stupid. Do you agree?
TRANSLATOR: I . . .
MARGO: Shhh. I'm being kidnapped.
TRANSLATOR: That's, uh . . . too bad.
MARGO: They want my boyfriend to come for me.
TRANSLATOR: Where are they taking you?
MARGO: They didn't say. Oh, yeah—a hotel in Mexico. The Hacienda Ramon.
TRANSLATOR: What a coincidence. That's exactly where I . . .
JEWELLER: Ah. Here's the taxidermist now.
TAXIDERMIST: Listen carefully, so that when you bring me the skin you won't have marred all. In preparing lifesize mounts of men, a cut should be made from the throat to the crotch in the underbelly. Then cut in from the center of each palm to this main cut. Peel this thief's skin back, and off completely. Skin the feet out to the last joint in his toes. Proceed in the face area as for antlered animals.
MARGO: He isn't antlered.
TAXIDERMIST: Wash any blood off with cold water. Salt the skin thoroughly. Let it drain, salt again. Regular table salt will do. Diamond Crystal, for example, is fine.
JEWELLER: General, write that down. Diamond Crystal.
TAXIDERMIST: Do all this, and bleach out the bones. I will articulate and mount him with pleasure. Half now, half on delivery.
JEWELLER: Nothing now. I need to see the work. It's going to be complex. He won't be complete.
MARGO: You'll need to improvise.
TAXIDERMIST: Whose plaything is that? What is she saying?
JEWELLER: She has been refusing to accept her . . . situation. Her mind is playing tricks on her.
GENERAL: She's the bait.
MARGO: I'm a nurse in this clinic. There. How easily we communicate when we're in the same context. We understood each other, just for a moment. Isn't that fun. (*To herself.*) I'm beginning to think these patients are making sense. A bad sign.
DOCTOR: Nurse, relax. You've had a long day. Have a cigarette while I check the ward. The box is full.
MARGO: The darn thing's a paperweight.
JEWELLER, TAXIDERMIST, AND GENERAL: That's exactly what it is.
MARGO: Oh God. I miss my playmate. Did I tell you about him? The Unseen Playmate. You have one of those? You know what I remember about love? When She is disfigured, He blinds himself. And vice-versa. When He is disfigured, She blinds herself. Uh oh.

I better read my book. It calms me down. It's a silly adventure story.
JEWELLER: In the Book of Brightness, Rabbi Isaac the Blind mentions the two causations: horizontal or "one thing after another" . . . and vertical. There are no accidents, says Rabbi Isaac the Blind.
MARGO: I'm off duty now.
TAXIDERMIST: She's delightful. When you're done with her, perhaps I could . . .
MARGO: You. Go home. Sort the bones.
JEWELLER: The man in the next bed to mine has these dreams where he is in a dark place, red and green lights in the distance . . .
GENERAL: Ah! Service!

(*Waitress is heading toward them. Music. They're gone, and she is the barmaid.*)

18.

THIEF: I'm in this bar in Hermosillo. I couldn't stay with Deep Sea Edna forever, but I took her advice.
EDNA: Buy a butterfly net, and go to Mexico.
THIEF: Yeah. No one would think that a crazy gringo is wandering around with a ball of fire around his neck . . . You know I go through these little Mex towns and sometimes I think that these people sitting around the Zocalo can see my thoughts cause the stone is shining in my head and they can look right in and see it . . . and one of them is gonna say,
MAN: Beer, Señor? I myself am very interested in red and green butterflies.
THIEF: and lead me down this alley and a coupla guys with pigstickers are gonna emerge from a pink door while Marty Robbins sings El Paso and I'm gonna be in a big puddle of blood, and I'm not only gonna be there, I'm gonna stay there. So I'm a careful traveller . . . down through Enseñada, Guaymas. Here in Hermosillo, I got nervous. I hired ten guys to dress up like me, gave 'em butterfly nets, told 'em to go to the public library and carry books around town, so my image would drift confusingly around these dusty streets, past the statues of generals . . . Or did I dream that? . . . I'm in this bar in Hermosillo, the PLATILLO VOLADOR. Sitting at the bar next to me is a guy from America, fat guy in a gray suit, looks like a pool hustler from Indianapolis and I'm not far wrong as he's from Grand Forks, North Dakota. I open the conversation. How you doin'?
MAN: Behaving.
THIEF: And I gotta think about that one. I figure he wants me to know that right now he is not in a Mexican whorehouse, or chasing the waitress around the tables while his wife sits in North Dakota screaming at the kids. But he wants to *imply* that he could be going wild if he wasn't exercising

control. He's got the potential. A guy who knows where to find his pleasures . . .
MAN: Hey—Teresa, gimme another, will you.
TERESA: You got it.
THIEF: Then I understand what he meant. He just wants to tell me he's 'behaving,' like exhibiting behavior, like at the zoo—and implying that I should watch this with some attention and I might learn something. Just see him lift his glass, slide his elbow forward on the bar, sit back and breathe. Just breathe.
MAN: They could put me in jail for what I'm thinking about doing to Teresa, but they won't. They can't find out. It's inside my head.
THIEF: Yeah.
MAN: What's your line of work, Mr. . . .
THIEF: "Mr. Raven" I tell him. I'm a dealer in precious stones. He'd look at me like I was crazy, but he don't, cause he isn't listening. *He* wants to tell *me* something.
MAN: I been around the world. Three years in Thailand, two in Japan, I been in France, England, all those places, and you know what? This town we're in right now, this is the best damn place in the world.
THIEF: I think that one over. Well, I don't know, I mean, I'd like to be somewhere else. I have this girlfriend and I find this place a little scary.
MAN: You're wrong. I been around. I know. This is it. Best damn place in the world.
THIEF: Teresa brings him another, he tosses it down, leaves a pile of pesos on the bar, and stalks out, all before I have a chance to agree with him.
TERESA: Teresa hands the Thief a newspaper.
THIEF: Hey . . . Margo's picture. It's her. I quote. "The Oculist's annual trade fair and exhibition will be held, as usual, at the exclusive Hacienda Ramon. Miss Margo Lamont will present the Oculist of the Year award at seven in ballroom E. Party at eight." There's more . . .

(*All arrive at Hacienda Gate. Doorman. Changing vision of the Hacienda as Deep Sea Edna, General, Jeweller and Margo, and then the Translator arrive.*)

THIEF: (*Continues.*) "The Hacienda's electric garden is open to the public between three and six p.m. Displays of frames, lenses, eye charts, and devices for examination and correction will be found in ballroom E. At this moment, on the terrace adjacent to the main dining room, two men are deep in conversation. Continued p. 14, column 2.
TERESA: Will that be all?
THIEF: No. There's more. I gotta bring something somewhere. I gotta meet someone.

(*Thief is gone.*)

TERESA: Hey—you forgot your butterfly net.

19.

ZENDAVESTA: Have you taken the tour?
TRANSLATOR: Mr. Zendavesta, you said there'd be peace and quiet down here, that we'd have time to work on the translation. You've done nothing but dance with the wives of oculists from Detroit till dawn. You're never in your room. Look, I have to be honest with you. This text is either so corrupt with modern emendations that further work on it is pointless, or I am simply incapable of—
ZENDAVESTA: Have you taken the tour?
TRANSLATOR: No . . .
ZENDAVESTA: Take the tour.
TRANSLATOR: I don't think you understand. This supposedly third century B.C. text has a fragment in it in which a jeweller and some companions take a train ride. It's like translating some kind of grade B adventure story. This can't be *the* book of the Yellow Ancestor. Yet, there's something about it that . . .
ZENDAVESTA: These oculists all around us . . . don't they seem to you to be somehow—wonderful?
TRANSLATOR: Look, I've been trans— . . .
ZENDAVESTA: No doubt you're an intelligent young man, and I appreciate your efforts . . . but I'm no longer concerned with how they—end. Keep the manuscript. Translate it if you wish. Its secrets no longer matter to me.

I'll be frank. For most of my life I assumed that those men and women I saw around me were . . . contraptions, not people with feelings like my own. I planned to escape them by creating a universe of my own, and moving there.

But this convention has opened my eyes. I was sitting in the Tropical Lounge, in this very hotel, the night I arrived, alone. Upstairs, at the desk, the first oculists were checking in. The bartender was missing two of his front teeth. I had a stomach ache. Then suddenly, I understood the truth. That evening, in the Tropical Lounge at the Hacienda Ramon, by divine miracle, nerves of God had been projected into my body. God's semen, you see, in the form of divine white nerves, has extended down from heaven and pierced my form. Impregnation has taken place. There is no longer anything I want to know, or anyplace I want to go. (*Mrs. Lammle enters.*)

I have enemies, however. Plans are being made at this very moment to abort the sacred seed, by pumping out my spinal cord. This they intend to do by means of so-called little men, placed in my feet.
TRANSLATOR: You are totally out of you fucking mind.

ZENDAVESTA: Take the tour. I think you'll find it instructive.
TRANSLATOR: What tour? Where are you going?

                                20.

MRS. LAMMLE: Do you mind if I sit down? I couldn't help overhearing your conversation. My name is Mrs. Carl Lammle. I'm not interested in philosophy. I used to be, but now I think it's a lot of shit. I just want to talk to someone.
TRANSLATOR: I'm someone.
MRS. LAMMLE: Good. I'm here with my husband—Carl. He's a professor of the retina or something. Very disciplined, Carl. We've been married for twenty-seven years. Carl's a member of the Rotary Club, hasn't missed a weekly meeting for those twenty-seven years. He went to a meeting yesterday in Mexico City, doesn't speak a word of Spanish, and there were all these Mexican Rotarians saying things he didn't understand, and shaking his hand. He came back very pleased.

We have a son. His name is Fred, and I don't tell you this to make you feel bad for me. He was born with brain damage. He's 26 years old now. Carl goes to this clinic in the mountains every weekend, to shave him. Fred never recognizes him. I stopped going years ago.

You know, people say I look all right, but inside, I'm a basket case. Last night I woke up about two a.m., thought I was sick. I was covered with sweat, racing inside like a car engine when the accelerator's stuck. I even got dressed and went down to the Tropical Lounge. Nobody around but the bartender. Some Mexican song was on the jukebox. It made me cry. Sometimes I think that nothing's happened for the past thirty years, except inside my head, and that's always repeating itself. I used to write articles for magazines, and believed I knew things other people didn't know, and that they should find them out from me. That's a lot of shit—don't you think?
TRANSLATOR: I don't know . . . The most amazing thing about this place is that when I close my eyes, and then open them again, it doesn't go away.
MRS. LAMMLE: You think that's amazing?
TRANSLATOR: Well . . . yes.
MRS. LAMMLE: Fine. Ah. Room Service. I want to tell you a story. There's no point, really. It's part of my life and very simple. When I was a young girl, I got a job demonstrating gas stoves for the Magic Chef stove company. This was in the Depression, and people didn't have much money to buy food, much less gas stoves, and I was selling them in Oklahoma, which was worse off than most. But it was the time of the oil and gas boom down there. Lots of people whose land was crossed by pipeline were allowed by the companies to tap into the gaspipe for free. So they were a pretty good

market for the Magic Chef range.

I had a driver, who also did my grocery shopping and rented the town theatre, where I'd put on this cooking show. I memorized certain recipes and had practiced, so I did 'em just right on the Magic Chef. I'd pass the results around the hall on paper plates. Those people would figure a pretty young thing like me couldn't cook that well, so the stove *must* have done it. And they'd buy. I'd do a few simple tricks too—color changing scarves mostly. After all, it was Magic Chef. I did that for two years.

What do you do?

TRANSLATOR: I'm a sort of writer.

MRS. LAMMLE: Are you going to put me in a story?

TRANSLATOR: Don't worry. I'd never put you in a story in a way you wouldn't like.

MRS. LAMMLE: What way wouldn't I like? It's all the same to me.

21.

JEWELLER: General, the ballroom is ready. The party begins. When the Thief appears, searching for Margo, approach him cautiously. Some casual conversation . . .

GENERAL: Good idea.

MARGO: Yeah. Let's talk to him. I've got a few things to tell him myself.

JEWELLER: Soon, I'll meet him. I'm no longer sure what I will do.

A man may wander, unaware, into murky windings underground, from which he may never emerge. The Zohar tells of three men who determined to explore this realm of darkness. They descended. One still clings in terror to the wall near the entrance, too fearful to move—one went mad, and disappeared forever among the pathways of the black maze. Only the third, Rabbi Isaac the Blind, returned safely. He claims to have met himself, and led himself back to the upper world.

(*Music.*)

MRS. LAMMLE: The party! Everyone will be there.

TRANSLATOR: I don't feel like going to a . . .

MRS. LAMMLE: Come on. I wouldn't miss it for the world.

22.

(*The Ballroom. Music. All characters except the Thief appear. Cook emerges from his cage.*)

DEEP SEA ED: Edna!

DEEP SEA EDNA: Ed!

(*A stately dance, during which the Thief arrives, and places the diamond on a pedestal among the dancers. The dancers stop their movement.*)

23.

MRS. LAMMLE: Just how I like it.
EDNA: Right in the sight lines.
MARGO: Very up-tempo.
MRS. LAMMLE: Under control.
GENERAL: And on the level.
JEWELLER: Just how I like it.
ZENDAVESTA: Perfect. Just going through the motions.
MARGO: Exactly. I want my life to be so pure I'll get death threats from the public.
ED: You got anything worth safe-keeping, leave it with the Fat Boy. He never leaves his chair.
THIEF: I like to spend my money on things that disappear—liquor, food, drugs.
TRANSLATOR: Things that come and go.
GENERAL: Sex is barely worth dropping my pants for.
ZENDAVESTA: Just going through the motions.
MRS. LAMMLE: Up tempo.
ED: Under control.
WAITRESS: And on the level.
THIEF: Just how I like it.
ZENDAVESTA: Have you taken the tour?
MRS. LAMMLE: The flying figure of a mutilated man? Yes, last night . . .
JEWELLER: What a coincidence.
MARGO: Leave it with the Fat Boy.
WAITRESS: Is the guest of honor here yet?
GENERAL: Who is he?
JEWELLER: I don't remember.
THIEF: I just feel good.
MARGO: Why?
THIEF: I don't know why.
EDNA: Good feeling from nowhere, that's a sign of death.
ED: Right . . . things that come and go.
TRANSLATOR: . . . the flying figure of a mutilated man. Last night . . .
EDNA: Perfect. Just going through the motions.
MRS. LAMMLE: That's right. Certain portions of my brain are being held hostage.
WAITRESS: Red, or green?

TRANSLATOR: At this moment, a limping Persian is passing by the wharf.
MRS. LAMMLE: At this moment, a plate of food is being soiled by the shit of two rats.
ZENDAVESTA: At this moment, one hundred and one emaciated monks are holding up their broken fans.
JEWELLER: At this moment the black turtle climbs up the candlestick.
EDNA: At this moment, the bride is facing her husband, the old man is feeding his grandchild. The bottle is warm in his hand.
GENERAL: What a coincidence.
THIEF: Things that come and go.
MARGO: Just how I like it.
ED: Leave it with the Fat Boy.
GENERAL: I'm not interested in philosophy. Just tell me how it ends.
EDNA: I'm not interested in philosophy. Just tell me how it ends.
WAITRESS: I'm not interested in philosophy. Just tell me how it ends.
ZENDAVESTA: I'm not interested in philosophy. Just tell me how it ends.
MARGO: I'm not interested in philosophy. Just tell me how it ends.
ED: I'm not interested in philosophy. Just tell me how it ends.
MRS. LAMMLE: I'm not interested in philosophy. Just tell me how it ends.
JEWELLER: I'm not interested in philosophy. Just tell me how it ends.
THIEF: I'm not interested in philosophy. Just tell me how it ends.
TRANSLATOR: I'm not interested in philosophy. Just tell me how it ends.

(*Ride out. Sound out. End Ride.*)

VOICE: Those who wish to ride again, stay in your seats. A man'll be around to take your tickets. Those getting off, step lively. Exit to your left or to your right.

END SHOW

AUTHOR'S NOTE: ON STAGING *DARK RIDE*

The text of *Dark Ride* includes a minimum of stage direction, and a minimum of description as to set, costume, and design. This is for two reasons. All the necessary information as to place and the movement of actors can be inferred from the characters' dialogue and the stage directions given—and because of my wish that the play be adaptable and responsive to particular actors, directors, and playing spaces. The text should be thought of as a basic ground, out of which the staging should grow. There is no "right" way to stage *Dark Ride*.

Despite my desire for anyone working on a production of *Dark Ride*, or reading it, to allow their visual and theatrical imaginations full rein, I would like to make some thematic and practical suggestions.

The idea of a "dark ride," or carnival spook or ghost ride through a funhouse, where images and scenes appear suddenly out of darkness and just as suddenly disappear, is helpful to keep in mind: lights in the dark.

A cinematic approach, where scenes fade into one another, or are cut to rapidly, would also be helpful to think about—the blunter style of B movies rather than art films. The lighting should be hard and colorful, and jarring, like that of a seedy carnival: lights to look at, as well as lights to light the scene.

Settings can be simple. Rather than using large set pieces, place can be indicated by props that can easily be moved on and off-stage. The use of slides, film, and sound to establish place and mood is also possible.

The text also offers within itself many visual suggestions. Often, all that is necessary to establish place is the language alone. If the director thinks more of the techniques drawn upon to stage a Shakespeare play, soliloquies to the audience and all—rather than a nineteenth or twentieth century drama, he or she will be closer to the mark.

It is also of interest, in a piece like *Dark Ride*, to stage, in the straightforward way suggested, certain moments of thought or memory as well as, or even as an overlay to, the present time-place of the action.

Also, directors, performers, and readers should be aware that *Dark Ride* is a weave of tales, of scenes within scenes, like the facets of the diamond. That a scene is within a book, or a picture, or in someone's mind makes it no less "real." The "real" point of view is a shifting one.

The following scene list may be helpful as well.

ACT I

1. The Dark Ride begins/introduction
2. The Translator at home
3. Margo at home/at the clinic in her mind/with the Jeweller, Head Nurse
4. The Thief at the Embers Cafe/with Waitress and Deep Sea Ed as cook

5. The General on TV
6. The Translator again
7. Thief at the Embers/Deep Sea Ed and ticket windows/Waitress
8. The Jeweller in his office/with Thief
9. The Thief at Deep Sea Edna's motel
10. Mrs. Lammle at a lecture hall/all as audience and demonstrators
11. The Translator and the Thief at Zendavesta's oculist shop/occult bookstore/with Mrs. Lammle
12. The Jeweller and the General at the Jeweller's office
13. Margo at home, with Jeweller and General

ACT II

14. Mrs. Lammle's lecture hall
15. The General, Jeweller and Margo on the way to Mexico/train with Conductor
16. Deep Sea Edna's Shooting Gallery and Marine Museum, with Thief and Zendavesta
17. A café near Mexico City/Deep Sea Ed's ticket windows/echoes of the clinic —Waitress, Translator, Ed, Jeweller, General, Margo, Taxidermist, Head Nurse
18. A bar in Mexico—Thief and Deep Sea Ed
19. The Hacienda Ramon
20. The Hacienda Ramon
21. The Hacienda Ramon
22. The Hacienda Ramon—ballroom
23. The Hacienda Ramon—ballroom/end of ride

CLEMENS KALISCHER

SHEILA DABNEY, CAITLIN O'HEANEY, PAMELA REED, AND SUSAN BLOMMAERT IN "THE BRIDES"

The Brides

Harry Kondoleon

The Brides was first produced in Stockbridge, Massachusetts, by the Lenox Arts Center Music-Theater Performing Group (Lyn Austin and Margo Lion, producers), on July 23, 1980, with the following cast:

Susan Blommaert, Sheila Dabney, Caitlin O'Heaney, Pamela Reed

Director: Harry Kondoleon
Music: Hal McKusick
Costumes: Rita Ryack

The Brides was subsequently seen at the Cubiculo Theater in New York City on April 22, 1981, under the title *Disrobing the Bride*. It was directed by the author with Patricia Benoit, music composed by Gary Fagin, scenery and lighting by Loren Sherman, costumes by Ann Emonts, and performed by Ellen Greene, Caroline Kava, and Mary Beth Lerner.

© 1980, 1982 Copyright by Harry Kondoleon.
CAUTION: No performances or readings of this work mat be given without the express authorization of the author or his agent. For production rights, contact: George Lane, William Morris Agency, 1350 Avenue of the Americas, New York, N.Y. 10019.

Once upon a time
And because there is no way to tell this story without stopping to cry
We will interrupt ourselves many times and jump from one end of the tale to
    the other.
Once upon a time

A NORMAL BRIDE SPEAKING

Often I went to parties and couldn't socialize. I didn't know how to smile or even hello. I was normal and felt out of it. Dates became impossible. I spent too much time alone and soon lost respect for myself. I waited.

Then came transformation.

I met a groom and the groom showed me how to walk in love (because love is the gift of the groom) and talk in love (this is the language I had never spoken before) and sleep in love (the groom shook me awake from the dreamless sleep of my life).

But my story is one of betrayal for my groom took a lovelier princess outside of the city and together they went into the forest and wed never to be heard of again.

PITY THE BRIDE

Her tears made a kind of swimming pool near the gates of the palace
And those to whom the broken heart was a mystery came there to swim when
    the weather got warm

And they pointed to her shadow dragging behind the trees,
 "There's the unwed bride—pity her and move on."
Pity her and move on—they made a folk song and sang it in taverns over beer and whiskey,
Pity her and move on—scrawled on the whitewashed outhouses and the magistrate's office.

    That there was to be no pleasure, no happiness for me I accepted years ago. I sat as a child with that fact in my lap and I lumped it with the other stuffed things children hold to distract themselves.
    When I complained to friends of my loneliness and unwillingness to settle for the scraps that fell from their own celebrations, they hugged me (the way you hug something repugnant which you have grown used to and taught yourself to believe is not repugnant but nevertheless hold back from and yes even flinch and wince)—with this hug I receive the love of friends, the charitable taking away and taking away and taking away.

I will devote myself to the groom, I said to myself,
And I will spend the long hours of his absence
Writing poems to him.
He will become jealous of the poems I write
And I will stop writing poems and make us dinner.
But he will say I am too fat

                                                               ("You're too fat!")

And I will stop eating
And grow thin as a stem, blooming at the neck,
In love with the groom.
But he will say that I have grown too thin

                                                             ("You're too thin!")

That I look like a string bean

                                        ("You look like a string bean!")

And I will eat rapidly, eat to gain
And diet to lose

                                                                 ("Gain!
                                                                   Lose!
                                                                   Gain!
                                                                   Lose!")

Again:
You said I was too big in the places I should be small
And too small in the places I should be big
So I made my big places small
And my small places big
And still you did not love me.

You said my voice was too high and irritated your rest.
I dropped my voice and spoke low and slow
And you said you couldn't hear me
That what you heard sounded false
And that I was wearing a mask.
When I told you that my mask was what kept me from falling apart at your feet
You said that while I was down there I could shine your shoes.

During the sex act there is a moment—some moments—brief and ecstatic—of unconsciousness. It is this unconsciousness I wish for in every moment of the day.

I can't come for you anymore
I did come once many times
I kept coming
I came so much so often and so far for you
I can't ever get back to where I started from
Now I want you to come claim the things you robbed
My tongue—cut it off—use that scissor, your mouth
My eyes, lips, arms, legs—all twin things of the body—chop them out and off—get rid of them
Next time before you go—before you leave the room without evidence, traces or clues—the weapon in your own pocket—leave some scrap of me behind—some small scrap for the dogs and cats,
They like to sniff at things that have sunk this low.

THE VISITATION OF THE TWO HEADED BRIDE

I was not always like this: mean and evil
The one pointing out the bad side of things
Once
I was beautiful
And sat on a windowsill
Looking out towards apple trees
Counting the ways
Wishing on a star
Mapping my own possibilities.

Something happened to me.

After that I began to see things as
Sour and unhappy.
I became ironic

And spoke as if all the things that were wounding me were amusing me.
Where I wasn't invited to parties I was suddenly invited to parties.
Where I was not spoken to or sought for advice and comfort
   I became a new source of advice and comfort.
Where I was hideous and uncourtable
   I became the fashionable friend
     to be carried like an expensive watch
     to be held, looked at and sought after
     during times of both crisis and felicitation.
Where I was the scorned, the hairy scorpion,
   the scabby old witch of a German fairy tale,
   I became the pleasing godmother,
   the well of wishes.

CONJURING THE GROOM AND DISROBING THE BRIDE

Be be be be my my my everything everything
Be the wall that keeps me from myself
Be every treachery I am afraid of
Be my father right before I realize what he does with my mother
Be my school teacher who has no life outside the classroom and whose only joy
   comes from putting stars on top of my compositions
Be God before planned obsolescence and before all the sadistic holidays
   invented for him
Be the sun and the river without particular meaning or sacrifice.

Love you
Love me
Love
You know that deep down in my heart I love you
Fuck love
You know that deep down
Fuck love
You know that

   Once upon a time a groom—that's me!—came riding on his own horse. Lo! he spotted a fair maiden, her skin a beautiful brown or white or yellow or red or black depending upon what I'm in the mood for that afternoon—I wear what he—the groom—is in the mood for . . . "Oh! fair maiden of multicolored skin, of hair and eyes worthy of the Uffizi, may I stop by this clearing and collect a posy of wild flowers to present to your fair nose?"
   "Oh do!" says the bride, already a little wet, a little anxious, already turning the present into the past by mentally describing this happening to her sisters who are less beautiful and stay at home with handicrafts and sketch pads.

"Oh do!" says the princess, already sizing up the groom beneath his tight doublet, his tight tunic, his tight tights. Already she is imagining his magic stick, describing it to her sisters who themselves will make quick sketches of the unseen instrument, exaggerating their sister's already exaggerated words. "Oh do!" says the bride, "Oh do! Do!" And the groom picks the sweet things—baby's breath, bachelor buttons and briar roses. "The scent will knock her out," he thinks to himself, already rather horny himself, already mentally unbuttoning the bride, picturing her high firm tits popping from their bondage into the sunlight, furry stingless bees resting on her tall dark nipples, and, unhooking the fushia bell—her skirt—finding the honey nest, dipping the spoon, getting hungry.

And when the sun is up over the poplars, over the cypresses, over the maple, the short dogwood and the stubby bush of thorn berries, over whatever is handy in the neighborhood—when it's over that, the bride and groom, their bodies a little damp, a little exhausted, roll away from one another, away from this unhistorical history, away from the morning when everyone feels small and uncounted and into the afternoon where, unnoticed, completely and utterly unnoticed, noon passed, and already everything has been, has been, has been, has been, the crickets shoveling seeds into cracks they won't see in the winter, birds believing in nothing, abandon their twigs and leave town the first signs of snow.

"Oh love me forever!" moans the bride to the groom. This is agony for her, this sudden second sight—this seeing the forest for the trees, this unquenched fire in her heart. "Oh love me forever!" screams the bride, already picturing a white dress a tailor with twelve assistants will slave over, already picturing the tiered cake, the guests milling in petal strewn aisles—already she is picturing all this and—simultaneously—at once with the ecstasy of fulfillment—betrayal—betrayal betrayal betrayal—at once—here—now with the groom inches from her bare hip—she sees his disappearance, the broken promise, the imaginary fouled sheets of his new bride—the Other—the chamber they will retire to when she—if not restrained by her sisters and her I-told-you-so parents would have thrown herself head first down the stone steps leading to the altar. "Is there no sadder story than mine?" weeps the bride, her voice muffled by her gown, her face buried in veils, "Is there no sadder story than mine?—tell it to me—tell it to me!"

And the groom in another city in another place in another clearing with a new sack of sperm and another set of flowers to pull out and wind together, the groom grows mythic, larger, more handsome, not aging but evil, evil, evil.

"Dear God in the heaven of heaven alone with your scratch pad of do-bees and dunces, of goodies and bad-enoughs, put me on the happiness list and relieve me from this feeling of being leftover, warmed up by my own hands searching my own vacancies. Dear God in the heaven of good ideas, good deeds and sporadic miracles: do something here now for this embarrassed woman!''

The bride waits for a response.

Nothing happens.

"God works in slow and mysterious ways," says a twig in the glen.
"God has a pipeline to every prayer," says a kettle on the stove.
"God makes results," says an uncut diamond on a jeweler's felt.
"Pity her and move on," they sing in town, "Pity her and move on."

What happens when God does not happen?
We turn to the devil.
Turn turn turn turn.
"Unhappy person to devil. Come in devil.
Unhappy person to devil. Come in devil.
Do you read me?"

THE DEVIL SPEAKS

"Hello my dear how pretty you look in your funeral gown did your mother sew it for you? I love beautiful dresses fashion is a kind of hobby for me. Don't try to speak I can see the pain you wear it and it strangles you. There is no zipper or buttons and the hem drags on the floor. I know it. You see I am something of a tailor cutting sewing pinning. Let me help you take off the pain may I? Bad luck in love is such a heavy fabric. Don't you think? There! Aren't I helping already? A good girl like you—why all you need do is forget—here take my shop assistant. He's small and scrawny but all fine husbands are. Make him your own my dear. I never had a daughter but I like to think a pretty girl like you crying could be. Think of me sometimes."

THE ARRIVAL OF THE TAILOR'S DUMMY

Once upon a time
And because this story needs to be told sideways
As if it weren't happening, as if it were all an excuse to get together and have
   a good time,
Once upon a time
There was a tailor's dummy, a boy
Obsessed with the bride
And though he was spindly, unworldly and dumb
The bride, already an abstraction herself,
Took home the dummy

And made a home for the two of them
In a straw hut near a waterfall—la la la la

Once upon a time
And because there is no parable to tell
And no lesson to be learned but what we have to learn from our own brittle
    footsteps on the wet streets
And because in the imaginary city of your heart
There are people who look exactly like you—
With your color hair and skin and your voice and hand motions and change
    of clothes—
And these people can't sleep
They are up all the time, an involuntary vigil
Their eyes like blanched almonds
Staring at nothing
Fumbling with glasses, with keys, with capsules
Fingers tapping at a table in Morse code,
    "What is there to see? What is there to see?"
And the answer comes back from the next apartment,
    "Nothing. Nothing."
And because there is no custodian in this imaginary city,
    no department of sanitation
And the streets smoke and stink
And the breath of the inhabitants is short and unkissable
There is no reason to go out
The citizens live like prisoners, tapping and fumbling
There is no moral

Once upon a time
You dreamt of something great and big
    that would seize your life
And that in the present everything was wrong and insulting
    you would put up with
Waiting for the great and big
And when you thought it was approaching you—
    wavery, incandescent, rich with the promise of happiness
You held your breath and closed your eyes
Grabbing and hugging at your reward, your fulfillment
But in the morning, with the spine of your pillow
    ripped open and its cut foam insides clung to the blanket
    and scatter rug—this mess!—
And you realize it was only a

Once upon a time

And because dreams don't figure in a commuter's day
And because even though *The Interpretation of Dreams* is a
   landmark bestseller when it's zero o'clock and
   you can't sleep there is no book written
   that you want to read or can read
And because dreams let you go on
When you shouldn't go on
And because a short story or a playlet with fancy acts
   is only real for forty-five minutes
And right now your mother and father are sitting somewhere
   thinking about when you were tiny and imagining
   that when you laughed and cried that you had a personality
   and were not just a baby laughing or crying
And you can't feel closer to them by remembering that baby
   anymore than you can get back to a foreign country
   by holding a souvenir from the airport.

"Oh where am I!" says the vertigo of the bride, "This play is not about me at all. Every minute the prattle swims further away from the desert island of my tragedy, any minute I am to lose sight of myself and fall away from Medea or Clytemnestra or whoever I'm supposed to be, my white dress striped red with the culprit's blood, my hair frizzed electric with vengeance. What's the aftermath of a great passion? What does a powder room look like with bloodied daggers strewn on the pink linoleum? Who carries the heroine in from her aria? What sleeping pill does she take when the deafening applause rings on decades after the one sold-out performance? How many brides in the imperial and non-imperial countries across the world are watching television tonight trying to forget everything before learning it? How many brides—or for that matter, grooms—imagine themselves years later going over the mismanagement of their lives like some kind of store inventory where you discover the employees have been stealing for years?"

Once upon a time
There was a tailor's dummy, a boy
Not much of a date, kind of a lump on a stick
And the bride, fitting this lump on a stick
Into her pain, which by now was purple and green
Took the dummy as her husband
Compensation made the bride grow youthful and lighthearted
And she thanked the devil
Who godfathered her twelve sons who
Much later when they were grown, sewed dresses and waistcoats
In the empty mill down near the waterfall.

And because I can't say goodnight
When I should say goodnight
I stand here in white, a conglomeration of gauze for an imaginary wound
   inflicted once upon a time
   and the scab picked open perpetually
   and forever the same itch, the same irritation
   the same cry, the same pus even
And on some imaginary altar in an already
   burnt up and pillaged city I am sacrificing
   myself, my live heart pumping as if
   everything could be relieved by just
   repeating something often enough by just
   being persistent by just saying it out loud
   saying it out loud out loud.

   This is the part of the story where my unhappinesses are so great I want to die but I don't want to die because I want to tell this again tomorrow and the next day and then again in some other city and so in this part of the story, because my legs are exhausted from travel and I want to walk no further, I wish to cut my legs off but I don't cut off my legs because at the end of the evening I wish to walk out of here and into the street—"Then what are these lies you keep telling?" you say to yourself and at this point I become ashamed because I seem to be talking out of both sides of my face and I want to cut out my tongue but I don't cut out my tongue because it will not grow back and I must go on speaking because of what I have to say, what same message of the broken heart, over and over—indefatigable, monotone—and to cure everything at this point in the story I should take my two hands (which I have not cut off) and rip out this red thing in my chest—rip it out and up.

But then if I followed my impulses
There would be no entertainment
No brides in the bridal chamber
Unescorted, attended by shadows
Mocked probably at country fairs
And used as examples by mothers everywhere.

The show must go on.
The brides sit.

   THE TWO HEADED BRIDE EVALUATING THE GROOM

Once I sat on the edge of a bluff and thought all things
   eventually crashed between rocks and were lost in the foam.

That the sea was without conscience or pity, I took for granted.
I liked its green-black color and admired its strength.
I was a simple person and could comb my hair for hours
    humming one song to myself.
One day a groom appears
Changing the color of everything
Hardening inside the bride
Coming into her plans
Changing sea shells into split level homes
    pebbles into driveways full of children
    their round faces smudged with ice cream
And the groom panting and pressing his wand in her magic hat
    says, "Fuck me! Fuck me wild!"
And the bride in an imaginary sanitized heaven
    is hearing, "I love you, love you child!"

Where do the grooms come from?
What farm or palace breeds these tall men?
Legend has it they are all princes
And at age go outside their father's gates
    preening and posing
Making posies of the wild things.
And they appear on the scene of a girl's life
Like puberty, not gradual, taking everything over
Changing her utterly
The body speaking the foreign language of the groom
Fitting it
Moving around
Getting hot, cooling off.
A white dress grows out from her waistline
Making a skirt, a brassiere,
A white veil like a purdah.
A bride is complete.

WAITING FOR THE GROOM

A secret little bride who lives in the bride
Right now is riding up and down in an elevator
In the dark apartment building of her childhood
Each landing is a shortcoming
And the suitcases she hastily collected from the hall closet are empty
The dresses she had dreamt of wearing
Are laughing on wooden hangers in New York Paris Rome—

anywhere small beads are sewn into mosaics and shine in the night
Nakedness makes the bride frantic
And without trousseau or change of underwear
She can't help but review her faults:
The pompon ice skates she forgot in a friend's locker
    and never retrieved when the relationship broke—trivia
The blind date who ripped open a sweater
    popping the round buttons so they snapped like corn kernels
    against the windshield of the car—trivia
The knee socks which fell to her ankles playing exploration
    with her best friend when it was raining
    and their loafers made footprints to the master bedroom—trivia
All these clothes, this memory wardrobe, this unpackable luggage
    from an unreturnable voyage.
"Oh me!" says the bride, "What paper boat did I board with my
    hand over my eyes, afraid of the brown water, afraid of the
    grey fish, the snapping turtles, afraid even of my own
    colorless reflection rising out of the water to greet me
    with my own inadequacies made clearer, my own indecisions,
    my own desperate need for a connection, five fingers for
    another hand
In this stinking lake, still bay, or gagged river
Why can't I see myself alone
Completed by my own senses
Why does this shadowy figure follow me
Ahead of me
His featureless face hidden beneath a bridge
His strong arms paddling away from me
Towards the allusive Other
And my feet getting caught in the watery muck of these reeds,
Ladders to my face for mosquitoes
Their slender legs and fine stingers
Investigating my expressions
And drinking blood from me like desert crossers at the mouth of a reservoir
Boo-hoo!
Screams my night owl
Right before I kill him
I have grown sick from poetry
Of my own veilly image
Caught in the solitary confinement of artifice
The slow strangulation of activity
The hulabaloo around a pen
The flurry of notepads
I am taking my sour-faced muse out to the woods

Where I will hack her, hack her to pieces
Maybe then I will live again
Perhaps in a woodshed
Without a mirror or paint for my face
Iconless and not particularly at one with nature.''

THE GROOM APPEARS

To be perfect is to be desired by everything at all times everywhere
To want yourself even, radiating self, absorbing others,
Consuming the dull, the unfinished, and serving it back
    polished, glowing, touched by inspiration,
    by idea, thought, form.
To wake up in the morning and be me
Is not a sin—it's not even uncomfortable.
To think me vain is to boil jam down to nothing but a fragrance.
It is not unusual that I should think myself
    the one steady object in a time of depletion,
    in a time of minatures without standards,
    goals or achievements.
At night, alone, my body pleases me.
Having it under the sheet completes the concept of me:
Legendary, not criminal but not saintly
Neither blond nor black haired
Of no particular race or beliefs
Without attachments
Potent but childless
Happy but not smiling
Sexual but not insatiable
Smart but opinionless
Groomed but without fashion.
To be the groom
Is always to choose first
To say yes and no from a distance
To push away those who push
To select
To be without competition or critics
To be the first one out the door
To appear suddenly in people's lives
    and vanish abruptly as if any damage were inevitable
    but negligible as if the broken heart were like
    a Greek vase, better broken than whole,
    more authentic, more valuable and mysterious.
To be the groom is always to be able to get a good night's sleep

Never to be bothered by footsteps on the stairwell,
> rustlings behind the curtains of opened windows,
> the unlocked door creaking.

A groom is indestructible
And yet he collects guns and knives
Which he hangs on hooks over his stereo
The turntable forever covered by the same record
Playing over and over
The speakers unforgivable
The needle, cruel and tireless, picking up dust
And even when the groom has left town
The song appears by witchcraft
In shopping malls, waiting rooms and bars everywhere.
A groom is pitiless
As he should be
A groom moves on
As he should.

WHAT DOES THE GROOM WANT FOR HIMSELF AND HOW DOES HE KEEP HIMSELF FIT AND GOOD LOOKING?

Change change change change
Is the therapy for long life, eternal youth and days without boredom.
Become apathetic and good grooming becomes impossible.
Stay interested in life and it will stay interested in you:
> exercise, massage your scalp, get enough sun, fruit and
> raw vegetables, eggs, fish, red meats and wine.

Avoid bitter things and failures.
Always be clean and neat but never talk about it.
Always be loving and caring but never stick around for it.
Travel, change your name, inherit money, sell stocks, keep real estate,
> train horses.

Be athletic but don't waste your time with sports.
Know the arts but don't flounder the long hours in the dark concocting them.
Observe everything from a distance.
Fly lightly, land only for killings,
Fuck feverishly, nap and take cool showers.

WHAT DOES THE TWO HEADED BRIDE SAY AND WHERE DOES SHE COME FROM?

Sometimes alone in a room you say is your own
You cannot sleep.
Small songs with one lyric compose themselves in the night.

They say you are no good and no one will ever love you.
Pills don't help.
A drink makes the singing louder.
Cars passing over the gravel have a destination.
How you envy them
Those hands on the steering wheel
Those feet on the pedals.
An unlit room has one geography
Blackness and imagination.
A two headed bride is born there.
She's not happy.
She shares everything.
Four hands clasp a tiny bouquet.
No waistline can accommodate the hungers of two stomachs.
No aisle is wide enough.
No march will not seem ridiculous.
But a two headed bride sees things
   no one else can.
She can see everything in the world
   for its good and its bad
   and appraising it thoroughly
serves it back untouched.
In this way a two headed bride is a connoisseur.
That she cannot fall in love
   be unmindful and laugh in the harbors of picturesque cities—
These things do not bother her.
And if she is tortured privately
   by any deprivations
She carries the weight bravely.
And if poetic men should see the virtue
   of a two headed bride
Or if lesbian hostesses should make the two headed bride
   a guest of honor
Or if the president himself should sit her down
   to high tea in the green room or the red room
   or whatever color room he happens to be in the mood for
If these small rings should fall at the feet of a two headed bride
Her mission keeps her from picking them up.
A two headed bride knows that being is not having.
She knows that loneliness—and by loneliness I don't mean not
   having anyone to talk to when it's raining—but loneliness
   when telephones are black snakes with eggs, doors are mouths
   with open sores, streets buildings and people are crazy red
   streams of stiff kayaks and hooked fish—

She knows that loneliness is the natural state of man
    and that friendship, marriage and childbirth are just mirrors
    you hold up vainly for a minute, drop and spend years picking
    the shards from your feet.
A two headed bride knows all ankles are bound and to take the
    tiny step is to move even too readily and to stay still
    even is to crash up against seeds and blossoms.
A two headed bride does not need a man.
At night alone, after you've invented her, she invents you.
And although her nails are too long and she refuses to comb her hair,
    she's kind to you
And since she knows you are your own most diligent executioner,
    she plays pardoner, balm-carrier, Mary of the herbs and scarves.
She uses the meaner side of her personality to criticize others,
    to point out where others have failed,
    where others have given you the wrong change and then called you a liar.
Alone at night on the airfield of your unlandable self with the
    puttering motor of your own heart, a two headed bride is
    a parachute with a jump option.

The truth is plain.
In the bridal chamber there is nothing to do
But lift and drop the hem of an impossible dress
To make miniscule stitches no eye could perceive
    and no machine could mimick
To fuss with flowers, with veils, with small place cards for the unplaceables
To do all this without considering
The absence of the event
The cessation of purpose
The thinness of the hoax keeps even disaster away
And the steeple the bride stands under peeks over and down to her,
    incredulous, sacrilegious.
Oh beautiful things in the heaven of beauty,
    ignore all the faults,
    the missing parts and the repetitions
Accept this attempt into the hall of beauty
Accept these brides who went to the trouble of dressing
Accept these apologies, these confessions, these overtures one after
    another, these appetizers and dessert without a main course
I'm afraid it was left in an oven in a heaven I forgot to invent.
Hosanna to everything I ever forgot to invent
For they are lying in drawers, on shelves, or taking up whole showrooms—
    flawless, irreproachable—
Marry a dream and never wake up.

Marry a dream and know no disappointment, digression or divorce
Marry a dream—avoid the bridal path—
Marry a dream—marry marry marry.

THE END OF IT

Sun sun moon stars nature trees animals and people.
When everything is described to death,
Made sensible by the insensible combination of words and pictures
Made palpable by just sitting still long enough to take it in
Take it in:
The two headed bride marries the groom
Perfection and freakishness are a natural couple
They retire inwards toward the mountains
Bread and dairy products appear by magic outside their door
They never quarrel
Sexually, they are a fiasco
Too intelligent to be touched? Who knows
Out from cliffs appear maenads
(Some say summoned by the two headed one)
Who ravage the groom and put an end to him
The two headed bride goes back to the normal bride
Where they become one person again
Oh and more magic:
A tailor's dummy is transformed into a husband
Although they are not uncontrollably happy,
They live ever after.

THE DEVIL AGAIN

"Hello everybody, you know sometimes I get so frustrated and fatigued. Other times my heart gets so warm I want to gather children around me and tell stories. Once upon a time there was a sweet girl (naked under her clothes) who longed for a sweet boy (naked under his clothes) and although they loved each other not this much they kissed. Disappointment makes your hair fall out. Look at all the pretty things around you everyday."

END

RON BLANCHETTE

MICHAEL GRODENCHIK, GEORGE COATES, JENNY SHAPIRO, LESLIE HARRELL, AND JULIE HAY IN "ALL NIGHT LONG"

All Night Long

John O'Keefe

All Night Long was produced by the Magic Theatre (John Lion, general director) in San Francisco, California, on March 21, 1980, with the following cast:

EDDY...*Michael Grodenchik*
JILL..*Leslie Harrell*
JACK..*George Coates*
TAMMY..*Julie Jay*
TERRY..*Jenny Shapiro*

Director: Ken Grantham
Sets: John B. Wilson
Costumes: Nancy Faw
Lighting: John Chapot
Sound: Wellsound

CHARACTERS:

Jack, the dad, 43 years old.
Jill, the mom, 39 years old.
Eddy, the older brother, 17 years old.
Tammy, the older sister, 16 years old.
Terry, the youngest child, 10 years old.

© 1979, 1982 Copyright by John O'Keefe.
CAUTION: No performances or readings of this work may be given without the express authorization of the author. For production rights, contact: John O'Keefe, P.O. Box 351, Fairfax, CA. 94930.

ACT I

Set: The inside of a house. It's like one of those doll houses with shuttered windows and big rooms. There is a stairway stage left that leads to three rooms above: Tammy's room, Eddy's room, and the master bedroom. There is a landing running across and over the spacious living room below.

Below is a kitchen, stage left, with refrigerator, cupboards, and a large dining table. Farther down the left wall is a sliding door which is Terry's place. There are also a few unexpected places in the walls for entrances and exits. Down center is a couch and a coffee table. Up center is the front door. There are windows all around in the walls pleasantly spaced and large. There is an upstage right window which is fairly large and, later in the second act, is blocked up with a stone cube with the curtains drawn hiding it, but in the first act, it isn't there.

When the play begins it is afternoon and light is coming through the windows. As the play progresses it gets darker outside.

Eddy enters through the front door. It's just after school. He has his books in a book strap. He tosses the books on the sofa and heads toward the refrigerator.

EDDY: Hi, Mom, I'm home! (*He pulls out the fixings for an enormous sandwich and begins to build one.*) Had a hard day today. Georgie Gessel beat up on me as soon as I got in the building. He told me to get off Buddha Row. I told him that I wasn't on Buddha Row. And that got him real mad. I'm pretty sure that he was thinking about hitting somebody before he got to school, especially me. I guess I got the face you like to punch. But I covered my cheeks with the sides of my hands like Dad told me to do and he only got me on the forehead and temples, sure protects the eyes though. Anyway, Georgie left in a huff after some of the cheerleaders gave him the read out. He got real red in the face and his eyes started to water and he snorted up his nose a lot and got me up against the lockers so that I made a big bang and I saw stars pouring out of my eyes and I felt all alone in the center of the universe like a big blob of nothing, shrinking all of the stuff of creation out of my head, and Karen Minataur bent real close to my face so that I could smell her perfume and I could see her big green eyes and her full red glisteny lips and her pearly white teeth and I could feel her warm, moist breath. And she said in the sweetest voice, "Are you okay, Eddie? Georgie didn't mean it personally. It's just that he's from the other side of the tracks and his dad beats him up a lot." I understood, Mom, I did. And I told her that. I said I had a lot of liberal guilt to deal with myself so I could understand the value of a psychotherapeutic perspective. And then she left and I heard Georgie's big Chevy roar off. I worried about her all day. If she keeps missing school she won't be able to go to Springfield Junior C.O. this fall and she has a fine alto voice. (*Eddy has now finished making his huge sandwich and does a California roll over the back of the couch and on to the cushions.*) But one thing I didn't do, Mom. I didn't cry. I know tht that might make me tighten up my facial muscles and lock my solar plexus so that I breathe wrong, but it did something for my leadership capacities. I *know* I won't go down in mixed chorus this year!

(*Just then Jill, Eddy's mom, enters through the front door with a bag of groceries.*)

JILL: Oh, hi, Eddy.
EDDY: Hi, Mom.
JILL: Did you have a nice day at school?
EDDY: Oh, yes, a great day, Mom.
JILL: Oh, that's good to hear. (*She goes to the kitchen and begins putting stuff away.*) I do hope your dad had a good one. He was so stuffed this morning I almost kept him home from work. But he wouldn't hear of it. He said, "No, Mommie, I'm going there even if I have to put straws up my nose."
EDDY: Yeah, Dad's a real spirit farmer.
JILL: Are the other kids home yet?
EDDY: I don't think so. I'll check. (*He shouts from the couch.*) Tammy? Terry?

(*Jack, the dad, opens the master bedroom door upstairs and steps out on the landing. He has a huge thumb on his left hand. Half of his face is covered with dried day old shaving lather.*)

JACK: Hi, kids. (*He twirls his big thumb.*) "Pluck your magic twanger Froggie!" Remember that, Eddy? And then he'd speak in that low gravily voice of his. "Hi ya, kids, hi ya!" Oh god, I loved that stuff! Have a nice day at school, Eddy?

EDDY: Sure did, Dad. How did it go for you?

JACK: (*Imitating Daffy Duck.*) T'ere did! Got my thumb th'uck in the th'ink. (*He holds up his big thumb and cackles.*) No way to earn a living.

JILL: Go wash up, Dad. Supper's gunna be ready soon.

JACK: All right, honey.

(*Jack disappears behind the door winking madly at Eddy.*)

JILL: (*As she continues setting the table.*) You know your sister Tammy might be on Candid Camera next week. They've chosen her from a field of ten. They like her voice and her posture. It could get her good grades in Make-up class and that's a red belt at beautician's school, especially if she perseveres and doesn't act immodestly in the courtyard of King Wen.

EDDY: Mother, what the fuck are you talking about.

JILL: Headaches. It's this eternal housewifery. I feel like a spermed horse. (*She stops and looks at Eddy.*) Did you know yesterday, every time I looked at you I saw a corpse? Do you think that has any significance? Or is it just my lunar menses? The girls at Dream Club said that I shouldn't pay too much attention to such things, that I shouldn't look at it directly, but with the sides of my eyes and feel it as the lather of rather large movements. (*She goes back to her table setting.*) They talk about all that yang and yin but I think it's really western motivation in drag. You knew that Freud's mother was a faggot didn't you?

EDDY: It doesn't really make a difference, Mom, she's dead.

JILL: Oh, but it does, hun, it does in the long run.

EDDY: Who cares about the long run?

JILL: You should if you don't, Eddy. It's not just rationalization, this thinking in large movements. No, no, no. (*She throws back her head and laughs.*) It makes everything so funny! (*She stops laughing and continues to set the table.*) But it's more than that. It get's you into the here and now. It makes you realize that you're not putting up with anything.

EDDY: I know, I know. It gives one a panoramic view, but who cares if I was your father in another life, Mom?

JILL: (*Suddenly glaring at Eddy savagely.*) But you weren't! (*She goes back to her table dressing.*) Understanding things in a big way keeps you from being a dip shit. Go wash your hands, your dad should be coming through the front door any second.

(*The doorbell rings. Eddy hurriedly gets up and puts the sandwich on the coffee table and hurries into the downstairs bathroom. Jill takes off her apron and brushes back her hair. She stops and looks at the hand she brushed her hair back with.*)

JILL: (*At first speaking to her hand.*) Children all around me. I give them enough room to drown themselves. That's the larger space. I just imagine a huge body filling a river basin, steaming with bio-thermal effluvium, baby smells and moisture. I wander about this body, past the amber oils of its antennae, thinking of it in the larger sense. How these viperous coils, these saffron fibers bejungle its dark pits and belched out genitalia and I realize that even God mumbles.

(*She throws open the front door. Tammy, the older daughter, is standing in the doorway. She is prettying. She's wearing a red dress.*)

TAMMY: I don't know what to say.
JILL: What do you mean?

(*Tammy breaks into a shrill teenage giggle and then just stands there silent.*)

JILL: (*Standing there very still, then . . .*) You're really making the place silent as a tomb, dear. Why don't you come in?
TAMMY: In there?
JILL: Yes, dear. After all it's your house.
TAMMY: No, it isn't.
JILL: But of course it is.
TAMMY: No, it isn't. It's your's and Dad's. But it's really Dad's. That is until you separate and then you'll probably get the house and a moderate alimony check.
JILL: You're probably right.
TAMMY: But it won't make any difference.
JILL: Why do you say that?
TAMMY: Because they're probably going to turn off the oxygen.
JILL: Who's probably going to turn off the oxygen?
TAMMY: The Telephone Company.
JILL: No, my dearest. They'll try to turn off the meaning and then you'll think you can't breathe, but you'll be able to.
TAMMY: You're not going to let Terry out are you? She's been letting the most outrageous farts and I can't stand it.
JILL: Terry's your sister.
TAMMY: So what? That doesn't mean I have to like her farts.

JILL: She's been having stomach trouble. You should have some compassion.
TAMMY: But they get into my clothes and the kids can smell it at school.
JILL: We all smell that way. We just don't keep our minds on it that much. Even Playboy Bunnies smell like that between their legs.
TAMMY: Well, I don't like it.
JILL: That's because you're still cherry. Well, don't just stand there letting the draft in, come in and wipe your feet. There's plenty of house work to be done for you to complain about.
TAMMY: (*Not moving.*) Oh, Mom, you know I don't really mind all this house training.
JILL: I know you don't hun, but we've got to spat about something, what's a mom and dot supposed to do with each other?
TAMMY: Mother, tell me the truth. Is the blood really passed through the sperm?
JILL: (*Smiling slyly.*) What do you think? There are no blood brothers, honey. (*She pats her ovaries.*) Come on in and play with the V.C.
TAMMY: The V.C.?
JILL: You know . . . (*She opens the closet door which is right next to the front door. A vacuum cleaner is inside of it.*) the vacuum cleaner. (*With that she simply turns the vacuum cleaner on and leaves it running there inside the closet and goes back to her table setting.*)

(*Tammy simply steps into the house, goes into the closet and pushes the vacuum cleaner out onto the floor and begins working.*)

(*The work and the noise continue for a while when the front door swings slowly open revealing a wan figure in a business hat and top coat. The hat is tipped over so that the bill covers the man's face. He stands there so exhausted that he seems to be leaning on his bones which just happen to be in the right place to support him. He teeters. It is Jack, the same guy who was upstairs just a little while ago only now his business suit and hat have replaced his thumb and lather.*)

(*Tammy, who has been vacuuming, suddenly looks up and sees the figure. She screams. Jill doesn't seem to notice a thing and keeps setting the table. Tammy continues shrieking and backs downstage leaving the vacuum cleaner abandoned and running. The figure reaches out to calm her but staggers instead loosing its tenuous self support and inadvertently heads downstage toward the vacuum cleaner, its hand still extended in front of it. Tammy, still screaming, pulls the vacuum cleaner away from the man by pulling on its cord, giving the impression that the vacuum cleaner is coming toward her by its own will. The figure stumbles toward the vacuum cleaner, hand out stretched, reaching toward the vacuum cleaner for support, subsequently following it and Tammy. Tammy screams and lets go of the cord. Jack, not by volition but by momentum stumbles into the vacuum cleaner, grabs its handle, and with one hand extended in front of him in a gesture intended to calm the girl, chases her about the room with the vacuum cleaner until it finally corners her and Jill*) *pulls the plug. Jack falls back against the wall.*)

JILL: (*Taking Jack's hat and coat.*) Tammy, get your father a chair while I fix him an olive equals vermouth and vodka.

(*Tammy helps Jack to his chair and sits him down.*)

JACK: (*Pointing at the vacuum cleaner.*) I don't like that thing. Put it back in its cage. This house is going to kill us someday. I suppose my son's in the bathroom performing his proverbial autogenesis. And my daughter? Have I Electra-fied you enough to help support an analyst? And my youngest, has it decided on a sex yet? And my ever present conjuga, have you licked my Swisher Sweets today?
JILL: (*Elegantly bringing him a drink.*) Yes, I have. (*She pulls a cigar from her bosom and gives it to him.*)
JACK: Jill.
JILL: Jack.
TAMMY: Oh, this is simply ridiculous!

(*She exits upstairs in a huff.*)

JACK: Well, so what?
JILL: That's what I say.

(*Jack picks her up.*)

JILL: Leave me off at the kitchen.
JACK: Okay. (*He carries her to the kitchen and puts her down.*) I'm going to wash up.
JILL: You'll have to get that guy out of the bathroom first.
JACK: You mean . . . ?
JILL: Yes, he got his thumb stuck in the sink and he's been there all day.
JACK: It's cool. (*Winks.*) Return to sender. (*He bounds up the stairs with lightning speed and exits.*)
JILL: (*Looking up after him.*) Clorine bleach, seven-up, poker, Skelly gas and Studabaker, that's what me and my Jack grew up in. (*There's a knock on the wall. She ignores it and goes back to her table setting.*) That's my last child, Terry. Jack and me, we watched everything change right before our eyes and no one ever asked us anything about it. They just said, "And there you go" and things got longer, and fatter, and pointy, and flat, and round and some lines got shorter and some got longer, just like the driveways. Up went the skirts and in went the pants and up went the kids and out went the bellies of some of Jackie's old army buddies and highways criss-crossed the country choking out most of the two-laners like old Highway 6. I don't feel any older for it, not in any physical way. But inside there's a longer staircase.

(*A slot slides open in the wall and two little eye holes appear. It's Terry.*)

TERRY: (*Drawling out her voice like Patty Hearst in her first tape from the S.L.A.*) Mom? Dad?
JILL: (*Still dressing the table.*) Yes, honey? Have you come over to a certain side?
TERRY: I think so.
JILL: Well, you'd better make sure. Why don't you wait just a little bit longer.
TERRY: Okay. (*The eye holes slide shut.*)
JILL: (*Speaking as she sets the table.*) Jack and me, we couldn't have another baby and we wanted one more, just one more so badly. Something to lead us across the border into middle life. But the doctor said that Jackie didn't have the juice. He suggested alternatives, but Jack wouldn't have it. He said, "That's what lesbians do." And we thought the subject was closed. Then one of Jack's friends, a lieutenant general in the reserves said that they had some interesting stuff left over from the space program and that it would all be very nuclear family and so we have Terry now, but she's not all the way through. I like to think of her as a girl. Eddy likes to think of her as a boy. And Tammy, well you know sibling rivalry, especially among teenagers. And Jack, well, sometimes I don't think he likes to think of her at all, especially when she's "all the way." (*A little bell rings.*) I think she's through. (*Jill goes to the wall.*) I think that's it, honey. Are you ready?
TERRY: (*From within the wall.*) Yes, Mom.
JILL: Alright, here we go.

(*She slides a section of the wall back and there behind it is the prettiest ten year old girl dressed in a sparkling silver dress. She is a radiant, smiling, perfectly healthy child. There are tinkling little music box chimes going on.*)

TERRY: (*Smiling sweetly and tilting her head slightly.*) Hi, Mom.
JILL: Oh, you dressed for supper.
TERRY: Don't describe things so much Mama, you give me the chills.
JILL: Don't go too far out, sweety, you'll cut your fingers on those diamond studded frets.
TERRY: (*Shivering at the image.*) Really Mother, you ought to take up bass fishing.
EDDY: (*Coming out of the downstairs bathroom.*) What's all this gobblie-goop? I'm never going to get any supper.

(*Upstairs there is a most horrendous clanging of anvil and hammer.*)

EDDY: What's he doing?
TERRY: He's ironing his shirts.
EDDY: Yuk-yuk.
TERRY: You don't believe me? Watch. (*She lets out a most incredible call.*) Hey,

Daddy!

(*Jack bursts out of the master bedroom and onto the balcony with a half finished steel shirt on.*)

EDDY: What's he trying out for, a razor blade?
JACK: (*Sneering while holding his nose with one hand and a sledge hammer with the other.*) Oooo, that simply stinks.
JILL: (*Who has returned to setting the table.*) See what happens when you get hungry?
JACK: Look. (*He sticks his thumb out in front of him.*) It went down. But the sink is still swollen. (*He gives a little laugh, then looks down at Terry.*) I see you haven't started to melt yet.
TERRY: Oh, eat it Groucho.
JACK: The other one was a song called . . . (*He sings the "Cream of Wheat" song from* Let's Pretend.) "Cream of Wheat is so good to eat that we have it every day. We . . ." But I can't remember how the rest of the words went.
JILL: Now we're all here but Tammy.
EDDY: I think that's a stupid name.
JILL: (*Calling.*) Tammy! TammyTammyT-a-m-m-y!
JACK: (*To Eddy, from above.*) Well, I think your name is sort of stupid.
EDDY: Well, "Jack" isn't anything to crow about.
JACK: It certainly has a lot more substance than "Eddy."
EDDY: YOU're the one who gave it to me.
JACK: How do YOU know that?
EDDY: Well, certainly, MOTHER wouldn't have pinned such an atrocious license on me.
JACK: What? With a name like JILL? I wouldn't be so sure about that.
TERRY: Oh for crying out loud, will you stop it?
EDDY: Keep your bionic nose out of it.

(*For some reason this breaks Jack up.*)

TERRY: Stop it, all of you!
JACK: Don't dislodge your magnet! (*He cackles.*)
JILL: (*Calling.*) T-a-m-m-y!
EDDY: (*Pointing at Jill.*) Hey, Dad, did you hear that? I think her voice is changing?
TERRY: This is going very sour.
JILL: Jack, honey, change for supper.
JACK: Aye, aye, captain.
EDDY: (*Staggering with laughter.*) "Aye, aye, captain," that's great, Dad.
JACK: (*Suddenly stops, his eyes bulging, his face red and intense.*) Do you think so, son?

EDDY: (*Effusive.*) Oh, yes Dad!
JACK: (*Making an especially big wink just for him.*) Then I'll be right down.
TAMMY: (*Appearing from upstairs.*) If you keep acting like this nobody's going to pay any attention to you.
TERRY: She's right.
JILL: Oh, there you are, Tammy.
TAMMY: Mother has the right attitude.
EDDY: Yeah, check your stools for corn.
TERRY: Oh Jesus Christ!
EDDY: What's wrong with you?
TERRY: You're so gross.
EDDY: I'm so gross? Look who's talking.

(*Silence while everybody but Jill looks at Eddy. Then . . .*)

JILL: All kinds of creatures inhabit the earth.
EDDY: So?
TAMMY: Shut up, Eddy.
EDDY: What is this, Mr. Wizard time?
TERRY: You're a creep.
EDDY: Big deal. So "all kinds of creatures inhabit the earth."
JILL: And they all have REMS.
TERRY: REMS?
JILL: (*Still setting the table.*) Yes, Rapid Eye Movements.
TAMMY: Yes, I know what you're talking about. Like in dreams your eyes follow the images going on in your head.
EDDY: My God it *is* Mr. Wizard time!
TERRY: Shut up.
EDDY: (*Ignoring her.*) Everybody knows about REMS, except you (*meaning Terry*). You probably don't have any.
JILL: On the contrary, I know for a fact that she has them.
EDDY: How do you know? Do you watch her after you put her back in the box?
JILL: No, I can see her eyes moving now. (*Jill, however, is not looking up.*)
EDDY: She's not asleep.
JILL: So what?
TAMMY: REMS?
JILL: Precisely. And the tire is having REMS when it's squealing, and the rain is having them when it's falling.
EDDY: That's ridiculous.
JILL: (*She pauses and looks up from her work.*) No, ghostly.
JACK: Let's have some supper.

(*They all sit down to supper.*)

EDDY: It's about time.
TAMMY: Eddy always gets so impossible when he's hungry.
EDDY: That's because I'm part lion. (*He makes a growling sound and paws the air.*)
JILL: Are you going to eat at the table with us tonight, Terry?
TERRY: Yes.
JILL: Oh, that's wonderful.
EDDY: Does she have to?
TAMMY: She has a right to eat just like anybody else.
EDDY: Don't give me that right to life bull shit. Just because something moves doesn't mean it's alive.
JILL: Your sister is very much alive.
EDDY: Yeah, but will she stay in one piece?
JACK: I'm always afraid to eat eggs around her Eddy.
TAMMY: God you two are bilious.

(*Eddy and Jack elbow each other and laugh. Jill serves the food.*)

EDDY: (*Chewing his food with delight and surprise.*) What is this, Mother?
JILL: Jello.
JACK: Jello? It's absolutely incredible!
EDDY: I've never eaten blue food, there's always been red and green and yellow and white, but blue . . .
JILL: I'm glad you like it.
TAMMY: Where does it come from?
JILL: Skin, tendons, ligaments, the matrix of bones.
JACK: Oh, God I love dinner talk! You know at work today I had this most incredible dream. I think I could turn it into cash, especially with the information you have just given me. I dreamed that there was this paper that took pictures. You see, if I was to coat some paper with sensitive silver compound and then put down a layer of bichromated gelatin on it I might be able to produce an intense field of light which would act as a lens through which anything would be in focus due to natural photon intelligence. Mr. Nobel added a little sensitive silver to a gelatinous emulsion and developed gun powder. You see, light was developed! Light! Light! Within the tonnage of the nineteenth century are the seeds for the ship to the Omega point!
EDDY: God Dad, I love the way you pop your toilet paper!
JACK: Thank you, Eddy. (*They both laugh.*)
TAMMY: "Pop," how apropos. (*To Terry.*) I don't trust those two bastards farther than I can throw them.
JILL: Don't worry about it, they'll retire soon.
JACK: (*With a mouthful of jello.*) Not me.
EDDY: (*Copying his father.*) Not me either, Mom.
JACK: Rough and ready, aren't we boy?

EDDY: You betcha, Pop.
TERRY: (*Grinning devilishly above her plate.*) You know you hate each other.
EDDY: What? Me and Dad?
JACK: Me and Eddy?
TERRY: Yes, both of you. I'm going to tell you something, brother dear. He's been thinking of killing you.

(*Eddy's blue jello falls out of his mouth.*)

TAMMY: Mother, you shouldn't let her talk like that.
JILL: Well, honey, if Terry says something it's more than likely true.

(*Eddy is almost paralyzed with shock. He doesn't move, he just twitches, his face growing redder.*)

TAMMY: Mother, you just can't let this go on. Say something.
JILL: What's to say? This is between your brother and his father. It simply isn't any of our business.
TAMMY: Mother, don't say that.
JILL: Eddy has to take care of himself. My obligation is to supply the elements necessary for survival, not to guarantee it. Isn't that right, Daddy?
JACK: (*Singing the Air Force hymn softly with an absolutely serious face.*) "Off we go into the wide blue yonder flying high into the sun." How does the rest of it go kids?

(*Eddy can't answer. He is caught in a spasm of trembling.*)

JILL: Excuse yourself from the table, Eddy.

(*Eddy gets up and staggers to the downstairs bathroom.*)

JILL: Kids, I want to let you in on something. Movement itself is a living being and the being is only visible when something is in motion. So when you're lonely, just wave your hand in front of you.
TAMMY, TERRY AND JACK: Thank you, Mom.
JILL: Well, I guess it's time to move on.
JACK: (*Wiping his mouth off.*) I guess so.
TERRY: Help you clean the table?
JILL: Oh, that would be nice.

(*They begin clearing the table which is piled high with dishes.*)

TAMMY: Dad, should we sit together?
JACK: I think that would be all right. What do you think?

TAMMY: (*Putting her arm around Jack's shoulder.*) Do you think we ought to talk about things, Daddy?
JACK: Yes, or we can watch the television set.
TAMMY: And we could laugh together at the jokes on it.
JACK: You're not a kiddin'.
TERRY: Mom, what's the clone of crash?
JILL: (*After an appropriate period of silence.*) Why do you ask, honey?
TERRY: Because I dreamed about it last night.
JILL: About the clone of crash?
TERRY: Yes. I dreamed that I was inside of this absolutely yellow yellow room and there was a black curtain that went from the ceiling down to the floor. (*She turns to Jack and Tammy.*) You two don't have to listen to this.

(*Tammy and Jack of course turn around and begin listening.*)

TERRY: (*Turning back to her mother.*) And this curtain, this black curtain had these waves in it that moved up from the floor to the ceiling. They did it wth a strange indescribable motion like . . . like . . . they were going poo-poo. And there was someone behind them because I could hear him clear his throat. And then he sniffed a couple of times and said real officially, "And now . . . here's Egg Yoke, the Clown."

(*Suddenly she starts scratching her head, but it is a peculiar action for it seems as if the hand itself is moving of its own accord. She begins whimpering as the hand scratches. The scratching becomes more intense until she is almost dancing, all the while she murmurs helplessly: "Mommy, Mommy" . . .*)

JILL: Terry! Terry, what's the matter? What's happening?

(*Jack and Tammy are totally aghast.*)

TERRY: (*Her hands scratch the space a few inches from her head while the rest of her body bobbles up and down.*) And then the man's voice came again from behind the curtain and it said, "Come on you little phlegmer cough-it-up-cough-it-up." (*In anguish but unable to stop dancing and quaking.*) Oh, and Mommy! I did!! I did and I did and I did and this black and yellow pointy clown man popped out and swept it up as it came out of my throat and fell on the floor and he kept on sweeping real fast and he always seemed to be right next to me even when he was across the room! Oh, Mommy! Mommy!
JILL: Jack, do something!
JACK: What can I do?

(*Jack rushes toward her.*)

TERRY: (*Suddenly speaking with an entirely new voice, a voice filled with such authority that it stops Jack in his tracks.*) Don't touch me, you jerk! (*Then, just as abruptly she is flung back into her fit.*) "Oh God! Oh God!" I shrieked and then the ugly, pointy, yellow clown came up real close to me and I could smell him and he smelled like baby breath, but thick, thick, rich baby breath. And he said, he whispered, I mean, "What's the clone of crash? Don't jump to any conclusions." (*Then, all at once, without the slightest transition her fit stops and she is totally natural.*) And then everything felt good, and warm and clear. And then the clown said, but he had changed. He had this wonderful apricot colored cloud in front of his face. He said, and he said it real clearly, he said, "Jack's not your daddy, I am." And then this verticle blast of steam shot up out of the floor and I woke up. And Mom, (*she stammers*) I just wanted to ask, (*she pauses and looks at Jill probingly*) are you my mommy?

(*Jill's eyes well up with tears. She looks deeply into Terry's eyes.*)

JILL: Yes, darling, I'm your mommy.
TERRY: Thank you. I want to rest now.

(*She goes back into the wall and closes it behind her.*)

JILL: (*Noting the silence.*) Well, now there are just three of us.
JACK: Yes, there are aren't there?
TAMMY: (*Looking at Jack warmly.*) Yes.
JILL: Let's all sit down together.
JACK: You're not going to finish the table?
JILL: I'll do it later tonight when everybody's asleep.

(*They all sit down together on a centrally located couch.*)

TAMMY: Each day, in every way, I'm growing better and better.
JILL: Each day, in every way, I'm growing better and better.
JACK: Each day, in every way, I'm growing better and better.
JILL: Growing nearer to God.
JACK: Growing nearer to the great white light.
TAMMY: Getting less tired by the minute.
JACK: Able to accept and reflect upon
JILL: . . . the minutes and the hours and the days,
TAMMY: . . . the incredible turnabouts
JACK: . . . which catastrophizes,
JILL: . . . and obliterates
TAMMY: . . . us in the end.
JACK: (*To Tammy.*) Speak for yourself.
TAMMY: I was, speaking for myself, that is.

JACK: Then why did you include me?
TAMMY: I didn't.
JACK: Yes, you did! You said, "us."
TAMMY: I meant me and Mom.
JACK: Why did you just use you two?
TAMMY: Because you're going to out live us.
JACK: (*Shouting.*) What are you trying to do, take the suspense out of things?
EDDY: (*Suddenly throwing the downstairs bathroom door open and shouting from it.*) You're not going to do me in tonight when I'm sleeping are you?
JACK: That's inconsequential to the situation as it is now! (*Then to himself.*) But it might not be. (*Then to Eddy.*) Listen, son, I don't want you to feel like a bugger under someone's table . . .
TAMMY: (*Wincing at the image.*) Oh, God Dad!
JACK: (*Wiggling his ears, puffing his cheeks and bobbing his eyebrows.*) What I mean to say is that deep down inside I want you to live a long time . . .
EDDY: But?
JACK: . . . But . . . I have very little control over that. You could be electrocuted in your pajamas.
EDDY: Oh, god, Dad, don't say that!
JILL: Eddy honey, you've got to be able to take care of yourself. Anyway it's beginning to get late. It looks as if Terry has gone to bed. Perhaps we should be thinking of our own.
JACK: (*After a decisive pause.*) Yuck.
JILL: (*Suddenly looking especially old and gray with just a hint of injury.*) What, aren't you tired?
JACK: Hell no! I just got back from work, had some supper, a little pause to reflect and now I want to go outside with my family and have some ice cream and night life.
JILL: What about Terry?
JACK: We can leave her with the Counter. We won't be gone long.
JILL: That's true. Some fresh air to cool the blood at the end of your cheeks, to liquify the eyes and clean the shining crystal. Oh God yes! I'd love to go out!
EDDY: Oh good fucking jizzum Dad!
JACK: Just like clock work. You kids are just like robots. I could have predicted your reactions. You are both in your element, the sluff. As long as you can look at the world in a sluff you feel secure even if it makes you feel crazy.
TAMMY: (*Whining.*) Oh god . . .
JACK: Well, we're going out. (*He looks at Jill.*)
JILL: (*Smiles back at him.*) Completely.
JACK: (*To Jill.*) Meet you upstairs.
JILL: Okay.

(*They both dash upstairs and close the door. There is a long silence. The air gets decidedly thicker as Eddy and Tammy sense each other alone together.*)

EDDY: (*His eyes downcast.*) You gunna go with them?
TAMMY: (*Her mouth dry.*) I don't know, are you?
EDDY: I was thinking that I might stay back and read (*He pauses.*) upstairs in my room.
TAMMY: (*Softly.*) That seems like a good idea.
EDDY: You mean, you like the idea?
TAMMY: Oh, yes, I think so. Yes, it's a good idea.
EDDY: For you, that is? I mean *you'd* like staying back and reading yourself?
TAMMY: Yes, that would be nice.
EDDY: Would you do it down here?
TAMMY: No. (*Pause.*) No, I would prefer my room.
EDDY: Yeah, I would prefer my room too. Do you think they're going to be up there a long time?
TAMMY: Probably . . .
EDDY: (*Jumping on her cue.*) Perhaps if your neck gets stiff I could give you a back rub.
TAMMY: . . . But they might not and then again, they might stay a little while and try to make babies.
EDDY: You know that they can't make babies anymore.
TAMMY: I know but they like to try.
EDDY: Do you listen to them?
TAMMY: I can't help but hear them.
EDDY: But do you *listen*?
TAMMY: Yes.
EDDY: Does it make you . . . (*He bobs his eyebrows once.*)
TAMMY: It used to.
EDDY: But it doesn't now?
TAMMY: Right.
EDDY: How come?
TAMMY: I know your father.
EDDY: You know my what?
TAMMY: Oh Eddy, women mature so much more quickly than you boys will ever understand.
EDDY: Oh God, here we go again! I suppose he showed you his cock?
TAMMY: He did more than that. He gave me an entire lecture on it.
EDDY: "On it" I'll bet.
TAMMY: He came into my room one night, right up to my bed, right next to my face and brushed my nose up and down with the front of his wool pants and I woke up and there he was towering above me.
EDDY: Oh, Jesus Christ!
TAMMY: (*Ignoring his retort.*) And then he bent way over next to my face and said, "You want to see my aquarium?" And I said, "What aquarium?"

And he said, "The one behind this screen." And he lifted the flap of his fly and showed me his zipper. And I said, "Dad, that's not an aquarium." And he said, "Oh, yes it is. It's a pressurized tank." And I laughed.

EDDY: You're full of it.

TAMMY: And then he said, "You want to see my dolphin?"

EDDY: Oh, come on!

TAMMY: And you know what?

EDDY: What?

TAMMY: I wanted to see it. I mean I *really* wanted to. I never wanted to see anything so badly in my life!

EDDY: Oh good god!

TAMMY: And do you know what he said then?

EDDY: (*Blending a sneer with a searing interest.*) What?

TAMMY: He said that the dolphin couldn't stay in the dry air very long, that it had to be kept wet. And do you know what I did Eddy? Do you? I fell in love with that dolphin and I kissed it right on its face.

EDDY: (*Incredulous.*) That's simply ridiculous.

TAMMY: But that was only the beginning.

EDDY: I don't want to hear anymore.

TAMMY: Why not?

EDDY: Because you always make up such stupid lies.

TAMMY: I do not.

EDDY: The last time you said he called it a "hover craft."

TAMMY: Well, it was.

EDDY: It never was! It never was anything because he doesn't have one any more!

TAMMY: But he does, Eddy! He does! And it IS like a hover craft. Eddy, it's like a flying saucer.

EDDY: Oh, come on.

JACK: (*His voice coming suddenly through the flung open bedroom door.*) Come on, let's get our clothes on.

JILL: (*Suddenly appearing in the bedroom doorway.*) Yes, all of us. Let's go out into the night among all those flat little houses until we come to an ice cream parlor.

EDDY: I want to stay back and read.

JACK: (*Appearing, grinning from ear to ear.*) You need the air.

JILL: You need the exercise.

JACK: You can get a stinky finger later.

JILL: Yes, Tammy, let the impulse sink below your will into the dark lake of your belly dowry.

JACK: Besides (*He pauses and looks about the house from the landing, then softly.*), this house needs a breather.

TAMMY: (*Suddenly looking about her at the house apprehensively.*) Oh . . . yes . . . you're right. Come on Eddy.

EDDY: *(Also apprehensive.)* Oh . . . yes . . . sure, Sis.

(Without warning and from an unseen signal Tammy and Eddy suddenly dash upstairs into their separate rooms.)

JILL: Aren't they incredible?
JACK: You know it.
JILL: *(As they come down the stairs.)* You know, Jack, Eddy's been having trouble at school.
JACK: What, he's not getting what they're trying to teach him?
JILL: I don't know. He never talks about his education.
JACK: Teen-agers shouldn't be cooped up in school anyway. They should all be sent to athletic farms.
JILL: *(Looking at the kitchen table.)* You know, I love that table.
JACK: Do you? I'll get you another one.
JILL: No, I think it's the way he gets along with the other children.
JACK: Well, he has a very nice singing voice.
JILL: Yes, but I'm afraid it's not enough to get him laid.
JACK: That's unbelievable! Where are people's values? And why hasn't he brought this up to me?
JILL: I don't know. I think perhaps he doesn't like you.
JACK: Doesn't like me? That's incredible.
JILL: Isn't it?
JACK: Well, what do you think I should do about it?
JILL: You could move out.
JACK: *(Laughs.)* That's a great idea.
JILL: You could also talk with him.
JACK: I do talk with him.
JILL: I mean alone, heart to heart. Let him know you care.
JACK: You know, I could do that. The only problem is that I can't stand him.
JILL: You can't stand him?
JACK: No, I hate him.
JILL: You do?
JACK: Yes, every time I see him I want to tear him limb from limb.
JILL: Well, then I think a private meeting is long overdue.
JACK: My god, it's been fifteen years since I've been alone with him!
JILL: Is that right?
JACK: Yes, I believe so. The last time I talked to him alone he was at least three feet shorter. Actually, if you want to know the truth, I'm afraid of him. He's so fresh and young and strong. I think he still hates me for beating him in the old days before I gave up the bottle.

(Jill is suddenly without warning overcome with fatigue. She lies down on the couch.)

EDDY: (*Comes out of his room talking.*) It's true, Dad. I'm having trouble at school. The kids think I'm too skinny. At recess they punch me in the mouth and they won't play with me even when I open up and tell them I'm lonely and need to be considered just like anybody else. They just sneer and tell me to drop dead. Yesterday I stuck my finger down my throat and tried to strangle myself but all I did was throw up on my shirt.

(*This breaks Jack up.*)

JACK: Come on downstairs and tell me about it.

(*But Eddy has returned to his room.*)

JACK: (*To Jill on the couch.*) I'll talk to him.
TAMMY: And me too, Dad (*she has appeared upstairs too*), will you talk to me? (*She exits also.*)

JACK: I'll talk to Tammy too.
JILL: Tammy too?
JACK: Huh?
JILL: Tammy too?
JACK: Tammy too.

(*Tammy and Eddy come out from upstairs dressed for winter.*)

EDDY AND TAMMY: We're ready.
JILL: (*Gets up exhausted and pale.*) All right, all right, if we must.
JACK: (*Suddenly shouting angrily.*) Yes, we must!
JILL: (*Flinching.*) All right, all right.
EDDY: Dad, I don't like the way you're talking to Mother.
JACK: Neither do I!
TAMMY: Well, stop it then, Daddy.
JACK: (*Still shouting.*) I will! I will! Just give me a second! (*He goes upstairs in a huff and into the master bedroom, slamming the door behind him.*)

(*There is a long silence.*)

JILL: I want to get out of here.
EDDY: I do too.
TAMMY: Don't reduplicate.
EDDY: I'm not reduplicating.
TAMMY: You are.
EDDY: Am not.
TAMMY: You said exactly what Mother said.

EDDY: What did Mother say that I reduplicated?
TAMMY: You said, "I do too."
EDDY: Yes, I know I said "I do too" but that was not what she was saying.
TAMMY: It was exactly what she was saying.
EDDY: "I do too" is the same as "I want to get out of here"?
TAMMY: Exactly, if you turn the sequence of the sentences around.
JILL: Children.
TAMMY: Yes, Mother, I'm not arguing.
EDDY: She is, Mother. It's part of a syndrome. She argues and pinches whiteheads in the mirror.
JILL: Children, put me on the table. I want to rest there and get my maximammery energy.

(*Eddy and Tammy look at each other alarmed.*)

EDDY: (*Moving toward her, but troubled.*) Are you sure you want to do that, Mom?
JILL: Yes, yes, I'm sure. I want to go where radiation is queen.
EDDY: But what it does to the bones, Mom.
TAMMY: What do YOU know about it?
EDDY: See what I mean? You're a compulsive bickerer.
JILL: Just lift me up and put me there.

(*Tammy and Eddy carry her to the table and lay her down on it.*)

JILL: (*Sighing.*) That's better.

(*Just then Jack comes in through the front door. He has shorts on and lather is on one side of his face.*)

JACK: Such interstellar heat! (*Seeing Mom and the kids.*) What's this? Has mama mia gone bongos again?
TAMMY: Dad, will you stop farting around?
JACK: Me fart? You know the daddy choo-choo doesn't fart, he "puffs."
TAMMY: Dad, you've driven Mom to the table.
JACK: That's nothing. You should take a look at this. (*He holds up a large model of the Saturn Five rocket.*) Those guys can hot wire anything. (*He crosses to Jill and bends over her.*) Hi, Mom, getting a little juice from the proverbial loins?
JILL: (*Smiling up at him.*) I felt a bit weak, Jackie.
JACK: If you don't watch out we're going to start calling you noodle bones.
TAMMY: Dad, that's nothing to joke about!
JACK: Why not? If you ever want a bit of your mommie you can pour her into a cup just like bowls of water and the moon, in every cup a smiling mother's face. (*Noticing Eddy.*) God, Eddy, you're getting hefty!

EDDY: Do you really think so, Dad?
JACK: Know so. Listen, kids, we're the reflection of actions done far, far across the reaches of time. We are the umbra of beings whose actions have preceded ours, whose actions we are in fact the result of. We are the feathers by which these awesome paradigms mount the just created heavens. When the alligators yawn, we yawn. That's why your mother's lying on the table. (*To Jill.*) Are you ready to go yet, hon?
JILL: (*Completely revived.*) Yes.
JACK: Good, I'll go upstairs and change.

(*Jack goes upstairs.*)

TAMMY: What a complete ass-hole.
JILL: (*Pleasantly.*) He is, isn't he. I've lost many a fingernail in him.
TAMMY: Mother, I've been meaning to ask you about that.
JILL: About Daddy?
EDDY: Tammy, don't.
TAMMY: Does Dad have an atomic penis?
JILL: (*Saying the word as if she didn't know its meaning.*) Penis? Penis? What an ugly word. Is that something you go to the toilet with? It sounds like "pooh-pooh" only lispy: "penis"? I certainly hope your father doesn't have a penis.
TAMMY: You still didn't answer me, Mother.
EDDY: Let it go, Tammy.
TAMMY: Mother!
JILL: (*Getting up from the table.*) Why don't you shut up and sit down.

(*Tammy flounces onto the couch, leaving Eddy standing there. Eddy starts to say something but Jill interrupts him.*)

JILL: Oh, you sit down too.

(*He sits down next to Tammy.*)

EDDY: (*To Tammy.*) I told you not to ask.
TAMMY: Oh, shut up.
EDDY: God, there sure is a lot of shutting up going on.
TAMMY: The trouble is there isn't enough.
EDDY: Want to pick my face?

(*Tammy turns her back on Eddy.*)

EDDY: See, Mom doesn't like that word either. I bet she doesn't like (*he silently mouths the word*) "vagina" either.

JACK: (*Suddenly on the landing, breezy, ready for winter.*) I don't mind the word myself, but I like the word (*mouths the word silently*) "pussy" either. Out we go!
JILL: Out we go.
EDDY: (*Whining.*) Oh God!
JACK: Oh God!
JILL: Oh God!
TAMMY: Stop it.
EDDY: I don't want to go out.
JILL: Out you go anyway.
TAMMY: Come on.
EDDY: I'm not going. My food hasn't digested, besides we'll be gone too long and I have to rest my voice.
JACK: You just want to play with your wopper.
TAMMY: Stop it!
JILL: She's right.
JACK: Who's that?
JILL: Your daughter.
JACK: (*Rubs his hand between his legs and then extends it to Tammy.*) Hi ya, kid.

(*Tammy throws her hands up in the air and heads stage left.*)

TAMMY: (*To Jill.*) I'm the only sane person here.
JILL: That's because we never bought you a pet.
TAMMY: Mom, do you really mean that?
JILL: I mean everything I say.
JACK: I know, that's what makes you so endearing.
TAMMY: That's what makes you so frightening.
EDDY: That's what makes you my mom.
JILL: That's what makes me so real. I am real, you are real, (*To Eddy*) he is real. (*She goes to Tammy, her arms open.*) And my beautiful daughter (*she embraces her*) is real. Come on, let's all go out together and stalk the night.
JACK: (*Opens the door and a gust of snow blows in. He stands there with an arm extended to escort them out.*) Butterbrickle, pistachio, rocky road, chocolate ripple, banana fudge, thin mint, strawberry, not to mention the sherberts.
JILL: Into the wind!
EDDY: Into the night!
JACK: Into the stars!
EDDY: It's cloudy, Dad.
JACK: But they're up there!
EDDY: That they are.
TAMMY: This is ghastly.
JILL: No, ghostly. The whole place is haunted.
TAMMY: Who will take care of Terry if we stay too long?
JACK: (*Grinning like a Cheshire cat.*) No one.

TAMMY: Perhaps I should stay back.
JILL: It's all right, honey.
JACK: (*Ghostly.*) There won't be anyone here.
EDDY: (*Who's already out the door.*) Come on, I'm getting frost bite.
TAMMY: (*Who is suddenly in tears.*) Good night, Terry.

(*The door closes.*)

(*There is a long silence.*)

(*Then the door in the wall slides open and an electric wheelchair comes out. A being in a strange iridescent body is operating the controls. It tilts the wheelchair down center and stops. There follows another long silence.*)

(*Then slowly the iridescent skin cracks and a figure emerges from within it. It is Terry. She climbs out and walks out onto the stage, beautiful and radiant.*)

TERRY: Isn't the world magical?

(*Terry goes to the refrigerator and pulls out a winged box. She puts it on the table and opens it. Inside is a large glass of milk. She puts the box back in the refrigerator and then picks up the glass of milk in both hands and walks down center.*)

TERRY: Aren't Dad and Mom rich? Tammy and Eddy really like each other. They're just teenagers. When they grow up and get a little more mature they'll depend on each other a lot more. I think Eddy's going to be an announcer on a space station. I don't know what Tammy's going to become. Oh wait! Maybe I do. Here it comes. Yes, she's going to become a personal psychologist like Dr. Amos. It's going to be very different, you see, the future, that is, I mean for people. I wonder where I'll be next year. Dr. Amos said I might last a long time. Elly said that I shouldn't worry about it. She said that once something has crossed over it won't ever leave. So even if I drop over dead right now it won't make any difference because I'll just be somewhere else. Isn't that wonderful? I think that someday we'll all just be big sparks bouncing here and there all at once at the same time everywhere! Whew! What a life it's going to be for us all someday when we all become light pulses.

(*Sings.*)
When I look into your eyes
all of the world opens.
Seas and clouds
and purple skies
break the wide world open.

Oh yes, oh yes,
even though your eyes
don't move anymore
and all the rest of you
drops away
there is the space
your eyes opened to

and you are there
and you are there
and everywhere I look
I see you.

ACT II

Silence. The front door opens and Eddy and Tammy enter, subdued. It is dark. All of the curtains are drawn. They switch on the light.

EDDY: I hate Father sometimes. He's such an oaf it's a wonder he can walk.
TAMMY: I know. Did you see mother's face?
EDDY: I tried not to look. Oh, Tammy, what am I going to do? I've still got almost a whole year left of school.
TAMMY: You? Look at me, I've got at least two years in this beanbag.
EDDY: Well, you could get married.
TAMMY: Oh, great!
EDDY: Well, you could.
TAMMY: Well, you could join the army.
EDDY: (*Aghast.*) Me?! In the army?!
TAMMY: Well, can you see me filling up some hospital ward with babies?
EDDY: Tammy, let's not argue. I think we're in for a long one tonight. Let's stick together, maybe we can put Dad to sleep.
JACK: (*Sticking his head around the door.*) Put me to sleep? Put me to sleep? Is that what children do to their elders in the Space Age? Why don't you just stuff us in a rocket and pack us off to the stars?
EDDY: (*Conciliatory.*) That's great Dad! That's where I want to go after school, I want to go up into outer space.
JILL: (*Peeking her head over Jack's shoulder.*) We're already in outer space, honey.

JACK AND JILL: Can we come in?
EDDY AND TAMMY: Why not?
JACK: Wait. Wait, let me do this.
EDDY: Oh, god, not again!
JACK: That's right again and again. Come my love, let me carry you across the threshold. (*Jack picks up Jill.*)
JILL: Oh, Osiris, what shall I do now that you're whole again?
TAMMY: Oh, how "cryptic."
JILL: Not at all, Isis sought her beloved one's creative member for eons.
JACK: (*Winks.*) And still does. (*He carries her across the threshold, sets her on her feet, takes her hand and kisses it.*) As the pomegranate sprang from the blood of Dionysus, the anemones from Adonis and the violet from Attis, so doth my bright green poplar tremble by the side of your moony stream.
EEDY: Whew! Did you hear that?
TAMMY: (*Disgusted.*) Yes.
EDDY: Oh, Dad, say it again.
JACK: (*Worried.*) What time is it?
EDDY: Ten thirty.
JACK: (*Relieved.*) The bright hour just before the work force slumbers. What shall we do, watch the news with the vast incredible collective?
TAMMY: I don't know. I think I want to go to bed before the rest of them.
JACK: (*Sweetly.*) Oh, no you don't! You shall not escape the love light of our circle.
JILL: (*Gazing at her knowingly.*) I think perhaps she doesn't want to escape the love light of her own circle.
EDDY: (*Blushing.*) Woowee, did you hear that?
JACK: That's your mom, boy.
TAMMY: Why are you always making me out to be the ninny?
JILL: I don't think anyone's trying to make you out a ninny.
JACK: I'm not.
EDDY: If you want to know the truth, I think that you ninny out whenever Dad's around.
TAMMY: I don't like standing here being discussed.
JILL: Well, you did just bring yourself up for discussion.
TAMMY: I did not. I just made a statement about how you treat me.
JACK: We treat you fine.
EDDY: We treat you fine.
JILL: We treat you fine.
TAMMY: (*Screaming.*) You do not treat me fine!
EDDY: Wow, that's incredible, sis, you're having a crisis!
TAMMY: I'm *not* having a crisis!
JILL: Tammy, move to the other side of the room.
TAMMY: What? (*Alarmed.*) Why?
JILL: (*Seems to be speaking against her will and in Jack's voice.*) Just do what your

mom says. (*Tammy, aghast, puts her hand over her mouth.*)
EDDY: (*Speaking in Jack's voice.*) Wow, you talked like Dad just then! (*With Jack's intonations and a strange gleam in his eye.*) You never know what your friends might turn into. (*Startled by the voice.*) So did I!
JACK: You do look strange, kid.
EDDY: Do I? (*Looking strange.*) How do I look strange?
JILL: Tammy, you come over by me.

(*Tammy starts and moves quickly next to Jill.*)

EDDY: What about me? Can I come over by you too?
JACK: Yes, what about us, can we come over there too?
JILL: (*Steely-eyed and firm.*) No, you two stay over there.
EDDY: I'm lonely. (*To Jack.*) Can I stand next to you?
JACK: Me? Yes, you can stand right next to me. You can stand on top of me if you like.
EDDY: Thank you.

(*They stand next to each other shoulder to shoulder with glowing eyes. As they stand there they sway slightly.*)

(*Tammy starts to say something but Jill puts her hand over her mouth.*)

EDDY AND JACK: (*Wagging their fingers at the same time at Tammy and chanting.*) No, no, no, no-no-no.
EDDY: (*Pointing at himself.*) He can't stand you.
JILL AND JACK: (*Jill mouths while he speaks.*) But I can.
JILL: Spoke too soon
EDDY: Mom,
JACK: I think we caught ya.

(*Tammy starts to say something but Jill and Jack stop her.*)

JILL: You'd better not stand too close to me, either.

(*Tammy shrieks.*)

JACK: Don't get freaked honey, we've just lost each other for a moment.

(*Tammy is now separated from Jack, Jill, and Eddy. Eddy jumps into the space between them and begins doing a soft-shoe while Jill speaks and Jack mouths her words. It's all kind of wobbly.*)

JACK AND JILL: (*Jack mouths while Jill speaks.*) You're on the other side, honey.

Just say something. Just speak up and the bad, bad movie will stop.

(*Tammy tries to speak. Her mouth moves, she gesticulates, but no sound comes out.*)

(*Suddenly they move towards Tammy.*)

(*Tammy screams.*)

(*They scream.*)

JACK: (*Mouthing while Jill speaks.*) Didn't quite make it honey, let's try it again.
EDDY: She won't talk because she doesn't like me.
JACK: She don't like me either.
JILL: Oh, stop it both of you. She's just a little alienated.
JACK: (*Shouting childishly.*) She doesn't like me!
EDDY: (*Buries his head in his hands and begins sobbing.*) She don't like me neither!
JILL: She does too.
EDDY: (*Speaking in Tammy's voice.*) "I do, Mother, I do. I like you. I like Eddy. I like Jack. (*Speaking in his own voice.*) And I for one believe her.
JACK: (*Beligerantly.*) I know, I know, but she's not saying it!
EDDY AND JILL: (*Eddy mouthing and Jill speaking the words.*) Shut up and give her a chance!

(*Jill continues to talk but Tammy begins mouthing the words.*)

JILL AND TAMMY: Oh Mommy, Mommy, please help me. Help me, help me.

(*Then Jack and Eddy join Jill and finally Tammy joins.*)

TAMMY, JACK, JILL AND EDDY: (*They begin very low and then gradually build to terror and catharsis.*) Hello hello hello hello hello hello Hello HELLO HELLO HELLO!! HELLO!! HELLO!!

(*The last "HELLO" is screamed and then breaks into laughter and they fall into each other's arms.*)

JACK AND JILL: (*Laughing.*) Aren't they great?
TAMMY: Oh god, Dad, I'm so sorry! I get so crabby.
EDDY: I do too.
TAMMY: We argue, and argue over and over again.
EDDY: Just like brother and sister.
TAMMY: No, no I was just on a trip.
JACK: And you got lost.
TAMMY: Yes, lost in hell.

(*There is a silence.*)

EDDY: (*Breaking in clumsily.*) Recapitulation, recapitulation, recapitulation. So much of it is recapitulation that I wonder how much we really do.
TAMMY: Yes, it's like a ritual.
EDDY: Yes, with the grown folks moving away from us in the fog.

(*Tammy and Eddy head for the stairs.*)

JILL: (*Stopping them.*) Where are you going?
EDDY: To bed.
TAMMY: We have somewhere to go tommorrow.
EDDY: And besides, you two should have some time to yourselves.
JILL: Why should we (*Meaning herself and Jack.*) have time together? Perhaps Tammy and Dad should have time together and you and me should have time together.
TAMMY: (*Her eyes flashing.*) All right, Mom. (*She looks down at Jack.*) Come on upstairs.
JACK: Me? Good God. (*Jack grabs his hat, coat and scarf and goes upstairs. Then, from the landing.*) I feel like a sailor that just got into port. (*With that he goes with Tammy into her room.*)
EDDY: (*Flushed and almost out of his mind with excitement, strikes a match and lights a cigarette he pulls from his pocket. He tosses the blown out match.*) You can call me Ed. No shit, you can.

(*Jill doesn't say anything. Instead, she takes out a bunch of bananas and begins chopping them.*)

EDDY: (*Descending the stairs.*) Don't let people dump on you, no matter what they say, no matter how they try to justify themselves, there's no excuse for them to dump on you.
JILL: What a bore you are.
EDDY: You wouldn't say that if you knew what was going on in my mind right now.
JILL: I know what's going on in your mind.
EDDY: Do you?
JILL: Yes, I do.
EDDY: What do you think's going on in my mind?
JILL: You're wondering what your Dad is doing with your sister.

(*She begins fixing a drink.*)

EDDY: (*Swallows.*) Is that for me?
JILL: No, this is.

(*With that she turns on the blender and it blasts over the speakers. The sound is so loud that Eddy has to put his hands over his ears. Jill is stuffing bananas down it. The door to Tammy's room opens and Jack comes out with Tammy's dress on. He is shouting for them to quiet down but can't be heard. Tammy comes out of her room dressed in Jack's clothes with shaving lather on half of her face. Eddy has fallen to his knees, his hands over his ears.*)

(*Jack finally pulls the plug on the blender and the sound stops. All four of them look at each other strangely. Then Eddy goes and gets the TV, turning off the living room lights. They all sit on the couch and stare at the television. The light flickers on their faces.*)

JACK: (*After a bit, speaking about the TV.*) This news is dead. (*Really wondering.*) Where are we, in Alaska? (*He gets up and walks to the front door, opens it. There is a huge polar bear roaring in the doorway. Jack hurriedly closes the door.*) Terry's sleep walking. (*Jack cautiously opens the door again. A little robot—tin cans and a coffee urn with little pig tails sticking out of a pointed dome—stands in the doorway on a little red wagon. Jack picks the little robot up and carries it into the living room.*)

JILL: Oh, I'll take Terry to bed.

JACK: No, let me. (*He brings the robot down with him to his chair and sits. He settles down with the little tin Terry.*) I remember when you were just a baby in a jar. Let me tell you a story. A long time ago before your mommy and daddy were born there was a huge carcass that sprawled over the aged topography of our world like a draping, endless, multi-colored cheese. Now, this carcass was in a rather advanced state of putrefaction. It was so huge that it was the sole source of our early atmosphere. The hiss of its decomposition could be heard even far out in space. Ah, but you know all about that stuff already, don't you? How the carcass was really a piece of god's gray matter and how when it broke down it taught all the amino acids to clear up and get it together. How there really was a god and the big bang was the sound of god's gun blowing his brains throughout the universe and that god really isn't dead (*pause*) yet and we are his lights going out one (*pause*) by (*pause*) one.

JILL: That's a terrible story, Jack. There isn't an ounce of truth in it. Put Terry to bed before her iron rate goes down.

JACK: It has already. Oh, your beady little eyes! (*He rises and crosses to the wall, carrying the little tin Terry to bed.*) Did you say "hover craft?" Yes, your daddy was part hover craft. (*The panel opens. He places the robot into the wall and continues talking.*) That's where you were born . . . in space like flies breeding with maggots falling from larval cocoons. Ask your mother. Your mother knows. (*Calling as if falling into a deep hole.*) Your mother was in pure balloon. (*The door closes.*)

(*The doorbell rings. Jack approaches the door. Then, he stops.*)

JACK: What time is it?
EDDY: (*Without looking at his watch.*) Eleven thirty.
JACK: It was eleven thirty an hour ago.
TAMMY: I want to go to bed.

(*Silence. The doorbell rings.*)

JACK: What time is it now?
EDDY: Eleven thirty-one.
JACK: A minute hasn't passed yet.
JILL: Well, go to bed.

(*Silence. The doorbell rings.*)

JACK: What time is it now?
EDDY: I looked it up. It was ten thirty an hour ago.
JACK: (*Disconcerted.*) That's ugly. That's really ugly.
EDDY: What's ugly?
JACK: Don't just ask me what's ugly, recognize it as such.

(*The doorbell rings.*)

JACK: (*Whining.*) What's wrong with me? (*He takes his dress off.*)
JILL: (*To Tammy.*) I'll bet that's for you.
TAMMY: I know it's for me.
JACK: It's a date, isn't it?
TAMMY: Yes, a gentleman caller. (*She crosses upstairs.*)
JACK: Tell him to use the window.

(*Tammy slams the door.*)

JILL: Now it's time for us to go to sleep.

(*Jack struts towards Jill. He takes her into his arms. They kiss passionately. Then . . .*)

JACK: It's time for us to go to the master bedroom, Eddy.
JILL: Goodnight, son.

(*Soft, sexual moans come from Tammy's room.*)

EDDY: (*Wide-eyed and left out.*) It must be pretty late, huh?

(*Jack and Jill cross upstairs, leaving Eddy alone.*)

EDDY: I don't want to go to sleep. It's not that I couldn't go to sleep. It's not that I'm not tired. I am tired. It's not that I want to stay up. There's nothing I want to do out here. It's just that I don't want to go to sleep. When I think about lying down it frightens me. I'm supposed to go upstairs and lie down in a dark room and wait to go "unconscious." And then maybe suddenly I'll find myself in some very strange place. (*Suddenly enacting a dream.*) "Here, drop down this hole." "Who are you?" "I'm your dad." "You don't look like my dad." "That's only because you see but a fragment of your dad." "What are you going to do with that rope?" "I'm going to kill you with it, my son!" (*Eddy throws his hands over his mouth and screams.*) I like the way it was this afternoon with the smell of Mom on the sofa and light streaming through the windows and doors, and salami, and baloney and pastrami and mustard . . . (*As he speaks the windows fly open and a bright, pleasant light comes through them, the light of midday.*) and the sound of birds (*The sound of birds comes up.*) and Benny, the postman coming up the walk (*The sound of Benny's footsteps come up.*) and kids playing outside (*The sound of kids comes up.*) and cars (*The sound of cars join the other sounds.*) and buildings with people sending information to each other (*There is the sound of typewriters and office machinery, drawers opening and closing, computer tapes rotating, etc.*) and jets flying overhead, taking people to foreign places (*Suddenly the sound of a huge jet starts at one end of the auditorium and moves across to the other end.*) and new things being built. (*The sound of jackhammers and bulldozers and construction work joins what has now become almost a roar, he has to shout over the noise.*) I don't like night. I don't want to sleep! (*He falls face first into his sandwich, fast asleep.*)

(*Suddenly the front door flies open and all of the daylight and noise flashes into blackness and a huge crash of thunder comes down. It is night again and there is Eddy, asleep.*)

(*Then there is again the sound of gentle rain.*)

(*There, standing in the open doorway are Tammy [in her original dress], and Jack and Jill. They are gray-faced [as if they were from "Night of the Living Dead."] They move forward, swayng synchronously from side to side as they enter the room floating on Eddy's streams of sleep.*)

(*As they move towards the center, Eddy's body stands itself up out of his sandwich and takes itself, zombie-like, to the swaying stationary group which waits for him.*)

(*The panel in the wall slides open and a slash of light falls across the floor from the unearthly illumination of Terry's abode and Terry comes out. She has transformed into a gray-faced zombie. She wears a little version of a Pope's hat. She sways her way to the front of the group. In her right hand, which is crossed over her left hand in front of her chest, is an*

Egyptian mace. Terry, now in front of the group, leads them downstage and then up the stairs and into Eddy's room. The door to Eddy's room closes behind them.)

(*Immediately, a light snaps on in the master bedroom and we hear Jill's voice.*)

JILL: Jack! Jack! Wake up!
JACK: What is it, honey?
JILL: Jack, I've had the awfullest dream.
JACK: Go back to sleep.
JILL: Jack, I think Terry's going to die.
JACK: How do you get that?
JILL: I saw her leading us in a procession. She was carrying an Egyptian mace.
JACK: None of us can live happily ever after, go to sleep.

(*The light in their bedroom goes off.*)

(*Jill emerges from her room with a candle and comes downstairs. Cautiously, she pulls the curtain a bit away from the window and peers out. Just at that moment there is the sound of a roving band of punk rockers chanting "Kick ass, kick ass, kick ass" etc. After a bit the sound dissolves and Jill lets go of the curtain and approaches Terry's panel.*)

(*Suddenly the panel opens and a green beam of light shoots out followed by a whirring. A sarcophagus rolls silently out of the wall. Terry's voice comes out. It is sent through a flanger. It seems to be coming from the beam of light.*)

TERRY'S VOICE: Come on in, Ma, the pressure's fine.
JILL: (*Backing from the wall.*) Terry, are you all right?
TERRY'S VOICE: I'm finefine.
JILL: You sound so strange.
TERRY'S VOICE: I *am* strange, Mom.
JILL: Where are you? It's so dark inside of there.
TERRY'S VOICE: It's all right, Mother, I'm not far away. Look.
JILL: (*She looks down cautiously into the sarcophagus.*) Is this my daughter?

(*Suddenly Jack pops up out of the sarcophagus dressed like a mummy and grabs Jill by the back of the head and tries to pull her in with him. She rips herself away.*)

JACK: You don't like us. You'd rather be with him upstairs sleeping and snoring and growing hair. You don't like the way we change our clothes.
JILL: I do! I do! It's just that it's so strange and you do it so often and so late at night. (*Speaking into the dark room behind the panel.*) Terry, you're breaking my heart! Where are you now? Am I ever going to be able to recognize you again?
TERRY'S VOICE: You *can* see me, Mom. I'm this beam of light.

(*Jill looks at the beam of green light. She approaches it and extends her hand to touch it, then stops.*)

TERRY'S VOICE: That's all right, Mom, you can touch me.

(*Jill hesitantly extends her fingers into the light. Upon touching it her body shivers. She withdraws her hand then reaches up again and touches it again, more surely this time.*)

JILL: My god, Terry, it's . . . you're so old!
TERRY'S VOICE: Yes, it was a suprise to me also. How do you like it?
JILL: I can't say that I like it or dislike it. It's just, just . . . (*Her voice trails off as she bathes her hand in the light. She pulls the sleeve of her nightgown down and bathes her arm in the light, then her face and neck.*) Oh, Terry, can you feel me back? I can feel you, every cell of you, a trillion billion cells of you!
TERRY'S VOICE: (*Also moved.*) Yes, Mother, I can feel you, I can feel you like I've never felt you before. (*Speaking as Jill bathes her face and neck in the light.*) Think of me as you would a plant cutting. Because one form dies doesn't mean that the plant dies. It simply moves from one environment to another.
JILL: I know what you mean. Only last night I lay in the darkness and I could feel that the whole thing was unknown, everything, every last part of it, unknown but real, so real and yet moment by moment unknown, even though it is all that I have, and that it is so strange, that it is so slippery and that it is for keeps.
JACK: (*Again popping out of the sarcophagus.*) Don't give me that greasy gobber! What would this reeking bitch know about class? I throw up on you, you sow!
JILL: I think Tammy's waking up.
TERRY'S VOICE: Yes, she is, Mother. And so is Jack.
JILL: I'd better go up, I wouldn't want him to think I was out grave robbing.
TERRY'S VOICE: Good night, Mother.

(*The sarcophagus glides back into the wall and the panel closes.*)

JACK'S VOICE: (*From upstairs.*) Jill? Jill? Where are you? Your side of the bed is cooling off.
JILL: (*Wiping her eyes.*) I'll be right up, honey. I was watching the punk rockers rove the streets.

(*She goes to the refrigerator and opens the door. Eddy steps out of it.*)

EDDY: I'm sorry, Mom, I was hungry.
JILL: You'd better get up to bed. If your father knows you're awake, he'll give you a middle of the night lecture.

John O'Keefe 152

EDDY: I'm not going to die at thirty-nine, am I, Mom?
JILL: No, Eddy, you're not going to die at thirty-nine. You're going to have a long, long life. Go to bed and sleep in the one you have for sure right now.
EDDY: (*Much relieved.*) That's great, Mom.
JILL: Don't explain it, you might run out of ways of looking at it.
EDDY: (*Said like "right on."*) All right!
JILL: (*Clapping Eddy's ass like a jock.*) Now go up there and hit the deck.
EDDY: All right!

(*Eddy dashes up the stairs and just before the door, spins and sails into his room and out of sight.*)

JACK: (*In his bed clothes.*) Was that Eddy? I've got something to tell him about fighting. What time is it?
JILL: (*Without looking at a clock.*) Three thirty.
JACK: (*Tasting what he's saying.*) I was dreaming about this curfew, this particular *cur*few . . .
JILL: (*Matter of factly.*) I don't want to hear about it right now.
JACK: (*Simply.*) Oh. (*He turns around, goes back into the bedroom and closes the door.*)
JILL: (*Continuing as if Jack had never happened.*) Terry, Terry, what's happening with you? Dr. Amos said that there would be changes, but Jesus Christ, if I had known what he meant I would have forgotten the whole goddamned thing! Give an idiot, a cannible even, but a neutron, a goddamned oversized neutron for a daughter, Jesus Christ! (*Suddenly she looks absolutely paranoid. She drops to her knees and folds her hands in prayer, and murmurs.*) Oh god, oh god! Let me know that all (*Pause.*) this (*Pause.*) isn't just procreation cooling on someone's face, my face, the Earth mother's face. FUCK THE EARTH MOTHER!!!

(*Tammy's light goes on. She opens her door.*)

TAMMY: (*Rubbing her eyes.*) Mom, what's the matter?
JILL: You worthless piece of shit! (*She picks up a pot and throws it up at Tammy. It misses her and hits the wall.*) You've made my life a walking nightmare!
EDDY: (*Coming out of his room on the run.*) Mom, what's the matter?
JILL: (*Thrown into an absolute rage at the sight of Eddy.*) You! You twerp! You don't even have the stuffing to be a homosexual! You pre-ejaculatory squirt! You're the one that really fucked up my life! When I was young I had balls, real balls, I had ten times the class squared than that muffin-faced mama's boy you call a father! You and that idiot winking at each other and letting chicken farts!
EDDY: (*Squealing.*) Mama! Mama! Don't talk like that, you make me feel bad!
TAMMY: (*Screwing up her face at him in an incredible knot of hatred, mocking him.*) Mama! Mama, you make me feel bad! (*She smashes Eddy in the face.*)

JILL: Let go of him! He's my business, you slut! (*She rushes upstairs and pulls Tammy from Eddy by the hair and throws her up against the wall.*) You stinking shit-faced little bastard, always stuffing your mouth. (*She pulls him down the stairs and into the kitchen.*) Here, you forgot this! (*She pulls the belt of her nightgown, stuffs his face into the sandwich and ties it to his face.*) I wouldn't want to send you out into the world unprepared.
TAMMY: (*Jumping up and down, clapping her hands.*) Yes, mother, yes, throw him outside and let the punk rockers get him!
EDDY: (*Through the sandwich tied to his face.*) No, Mama, please, don't, please.

(*Jill opens the door. It is pitch black outside. In the distance the chant of "Kick ass, kick ass" can be heard. Then she throws him out and slams the door behind him.*)

(*Outside the chant of "Kick ass, kick ass" approaches. There is a pathetic knocking and clawing at the door. The chant comes right up to the door. The clawing stops and all is silent.*)

JILL: Let's take care of this place!

(*Tammy rushes down the stairs.*)

TAMMY: Mother, I can't believe it. Oh, how beautiful! I've been waiting for this for so long. (*She picks up a pitcher and is about to throw it.*)
JILL: (*Stopping her.*) No, not that one. That one belonged to my grandmother.

(*Tammy picks up a coffee pot.*)

JILL: (*Stopping her.*) No, let's keep that one for ourselves, it makes the best coffee in the world.
TAMMY: Mother, we can get another one.

(*Tammy puts it down and grabs a handful of cups, dangling them from her fingers. Jill grabs her around the arms and pushes her against the wall.*)

JILL: No, not those! Those are mine!
TAMMY: (*Exasperated.*) Would you please tell me what isn't yours?
JILL: Well, hardly any . . . (*She stops and looks the kitchen over, her hand poised on her chin.*) I guess it's all mine. Let me see. (*She walks about the kitchen looking at various things.*) Yes, that's mine. I bought it when you were just a little thing. And this, this was given to me by your father in the forties. They don't make them any more. And this, well, this is just something stupid. And look at this. This is a picture of Eddy on his way to summer camp. Look at those sandals. Doesn't he have darling feet?
TAMMY: Mother, how can you stand it? Look at what you're doing. Look at

this crap you're tied to.
JILL: (*Still looking at the picture.*) You're not tied to anything, my dear.
TAMMY: I'm not? Then what do you call all of this?
JILL: Mine.
TAMMY: But what about me?
JILL: What about you?
TAMMY: What do you mean, "What about you?" Don't you care what happens to me?
JILL: Of course I do, but what am I supposed to do about it?
TAMMY: Mother, are you crazy? Look at all this junk! Do you want me to get caged in like you by all this clakkery?
JILL: Don't worry about my time machine, it's mine, not yours. You'll have yours when it comes. You'll have your own tools, your own shop. Leave what's mine alone. Leave me alone. This is my shop, my world, my place and you're simply growing out of it. But while you're here and eating my food, wash the dishes and sweep the floor and be nice to your little sister and your brother and Jack. If you don't like it, just go away and find a place that's better.

(*Tammy looks at Jill, her lower jaw forgotten and dangling.*)

TAMMY: I feel so crazy, Mama.

(*Jill takes her in her arms and holds her. Tammy is crying.*)

JILL: There, there, that's the way it goes, in and out and everywhere at once, like a vine chasing a spiral dream. First you want it and then you can't get rid of it like the sun just before eclipse. It's time to help someone.

(*Jill goes over to the refrigerator and opens the freezer compartment, exposing a huge breast with a livid swollen bitten up red nipple. She holds a large glass under it. A stream of milk from the nipple flows into it.*)

JILL: (*As the glass fills up with milk.*) You know the goddess Mut did this for Amen-re. He was the sun god who spat out the suckling Horus who later flew up and scratched the primal electricity out of the wind which polarized the amino acids into life. (*She puts her mouth to the nipple, sucks out a mouthful of milk and spits it into the glass.*) This top part of the milk is warm from the blood heat. That's what keeps Terry here—milk heated by her mother's mouth.

(*Terry's hand sticks out of the wall and takes the glass and disappears.*)

JILL: Sometimes it's hard not to give up on a child, but Terry will out pace us all. (*To Tammy.*) Now, you must go back to bed. You have your junior year to complete. As for me, I've got to go back up to my body and enter Theta sleep. Too much dreaming inflames the epitherial tissues and makes me morose and gives the ethereal body baggy eyes. Hold out a candle.

(*Tammy holds out a candle. Jill lights it and the lights go out while beautiful beams of light come out of the cracks everywhere, out of the windows and up from the floor. Jill's face is lighted by candle light. Silently she climbs the stairs. There is the sound of rain. She disappears into the master bedroom, closing the door behind her. Immediately a light in her room snaps on and we hear Jack's voice.*)

JACK: What time is it, honey?
JILL: A quarter after four.

(*The light in the master bedroom fades slowly out. Tammy stands in the shimmering beams of light.*)

TAMMY: I wish I could sleep at night. They're all out of their bodies away from the blood and the pain. I'm the only real insomniac in the house, my double seldom leaves the premises. Watch. (*She calls softly.*) Eddy?

(*Eddy suddenly comes through the wall. He is dressed in brightly colored ribbons and wears a silver bi-wingers cap.*)

EDDY: (*Absolutely natural.*) Yes, Sis.
TAMMY: I can't sleep.
EDDY: Neither can I.
TAMMY: Mother's been wobbling around down here like a cracked egg. She woke me up.
EDDY: Me too.
TAMMY: That's not true, Eddy. You're upstairs in bed right now.
EDDY: Don't mess with yourself, Tammy. You're liable to spike your jackle.
TAMMY: What do you mean by that?
EDDY: Short . . . circuit.
TAMMY: What do you mean, short circuit?
EDDY: Never wake up a sleep walker, even if they've been walking the streets for years.

(*He picks her up in his arms. She is fast asleep. He takes her upstairs. All of the lights fade out and there is the sound of rain and thunder. Tammy still holds the lighted candle.*)

EDDY: (*As he carries Tammy's sleeping body towards the master bedroom.*)
   I cannot fly, spirit, where you do not guide me.
   If you would have me soar beyond the storm,

Then must you beckon me over
And I will fly to you.
Raising my wings on a course beyond love,
Beyond all knowledge, beyond joy,
Beyond all human senses.

(*Eddy stands there before the master bedroom door with Tammy in his arms. He stamps his foot three times. His back is to us and we see Tammy's face lighted by the candle she is holding.*)

EDDY: (*Speaks while Tammy mouths the words.*) Mother? Mother? I want to talk to you.
JILL: (*From within her room.*) Can't it wait till morning? It's four thirty.
EDDY: (*Speaks while Tammy mouths the words.*) No, it can't wait, Mother.

(*Eddy puts Tammy down on her feet before the door and backs towards the wall and then steps through it.*)

JILL: Oh, alright. (*She opens the door.*) What is it?
TAMMY: Mother, I don't like the way you talked to me just now.
JILL: What do you mean, "just now"?
TAMMY: The way you talked to me downstairs a little while ago. About staying out of your life and that if I don't like it I should go away and find a better place.
JILL: Oh, for Christ's sake, Tammy, I'm sound asleep. Go to bed and let it wear off.
TAMMY: Oh that's fine for you to say. It's easy enough to cut somebody up and then tell them to stop bleeding. Mother, you're the only friend I have in this place.
JILL: Well, you'd better start getting around.
TAMMY: (*Aghast.*) Mother, how can you say that?
JILL: Tammy, you might as well start getting used to the reality that I'm just another person. One night I moo-mooed your father and got pregnant. The rest is goo-goo ga ga.
TAMMY: The rest is what?
JILL: Goo-goo ga ga.
TAMMY: (*Desperately.*) Goo-goo ga ga? Is that what you call my childhood? Goo-goo ga ga?
JILL: (*Unable to contain her laughter.*) I'm sorry, honey. But you have to admit it was a bit goo-goo ga ga, even now . . .
TAMMY: Mother, how can you say that?
JILL: Tammy, my dear (*pause*) grow up. (*She shuts the door in her face.*)

(*Tammy pounds on the door.*)

TAMMY: (*Hysterically.*) You slammed the door in my face! You slammed the door in my face! Goo-goo ga ga? You have no right to slam the door in my face, I'm your daughter.

(*The door opens. It is Jack.*)

JACK: (*Cooly.*) What do you want?
TAMMY: (*Backing away.*) I want to talk to my mother.
JACK: (*Low.*) She's in bed.
TAMMY: I don't care. I want to talk with her.
JACK: (*Turns his head back into the room—there is mumbling. Then he turns back to Tammy.*) She doesn't want to talk to you right now. She wants to sleep (*He grins.*) with me.
TAMMY: Mama! Mama!
JACK: Let's go downstairs.
TAMMY: I don't want to go downstairs.
JACK: Okay, then I will. (*He sticks his head back into the master bedroom and meows like a pussy cat at Jill.*) Meow, meow, my little pussy, be right backy-backy, honey buns. (*He closes the door and kisses it.*) Isn't it awful, the way we act? (*He pulls a flashlight from his bathrobe pocket and lights his way down the dark stairs. Tammy remains above on the landing. At the bottom of the stairs he puts the light under his chin and makes a terrible face with an accompanying sound. Tammy shrieks and sobs a bit more.*) Life has its ins and outs, its ups and downs, its weird caresses, its changing roles. (*He walks the rest of the way downstairs, and sits down on the couch and snaps on a lamp.*) There are possibilities within you right now that you have had glimpses of but have had no real idea of as they pertain to the fission of catastrophy. I liken it to a pony inside of one. Do you follow? A pony that trots and walks and gallops and sometimes races. A pony you want to call home to grain and bed down. It's your reaction to things. Do you get it? I know a friend of a friend who sat on a chair just like this one. He challenged his friend to talk him out of death. But there wasn't a chance either way, because his pony was on the way to the gun in his side pocket. You see, the lad was afraid to go home with his cold gun and see himself in the dark room talking to himself about how he didn't want to die alone. He wanted to give his friend a shot of his vision, and he said, "You give me a good reason not to shoot myself and I won't," meaning, of course, that he would do it anyway. And he pulled out this big gray pistoley and he put it inside his mouth and he watched his friend go white with conviction and hot air and right there in the middle of it all it seemed so funny, him with a gun up his mouth and his friend blithering like a spigot and he wondered what his friend's face would look like after he pulled the trigger and so he did, he blew his own head off. The bomb's inside, enough to blow the world away. And you can't ever tell when some little what-not might entrigger itself and turn the pony's teeth against its own dancing flanks.

Tammy, my love, my daughter, my dear little darling. Ride your pony good. Turn it into a horse you can depend on. (*Terry pops up from behind the armchair and puts her hands over Jack's eyes.*)
TERRY: Guess who!
JACK: Let me look at you. You're like a little ghost.
TERRY: I am for you, Papa.
JACK: You mean, you're not that way for everybody?
TERRY: Not for Dr. Amos. For Dr. Amos I'm a wish.
JACK: What kind of a wish?
TERRY: A wish for his daughter that passed over many, many years ago. There are lots of scientists' kids on the Otherside. I know because I cross back and forth. (*Sweetly she lets her fingers creep up his chest as she speaks.*) There are some very strange things all over the place and some people just can't get the feel for the inside of things. They have a ringing in their ears.

(*Just at that moment there is the sound of a distant, approaching siren. Eddy bursts in. His p.j.'s are tattered.*)

EDDY: (*Out of breath.*) Tammy's finally menstruating again!

(*Tammy gets up off of her knees and knocks lightly on the door to the master bedroom.*)

TAMMY: Mama? Mom? Mother? Dad told me the most wonderful story about a pony I have inside of me. And Mom, I feel it. I do! I do!

(*Jill hands out a box of Kotex.*)

JILL: Here you are, honey.
TAMMY: Oh, thank you, Mom. (*To Eddy, Jack and Terry below.*) It's a Merry Christmas! (*She exits into her bedroom.*)
JACK: What time is it?
EDDY: (*Just simply knowing.*) Five a.m.
JACK: It's almost time to get up.
TERRY: It's almost time for your sun to rise.

(*Jack crosses to the front window. He pulls the curtains back in a single stroke, revealing a solid wall. Everybody shrieks at the sight of it.*)

JACK: Don't get excited. I think we can handle this. Here, let me push against it. (*They push against the wall and it starts to move.*) Yes, yes, it's moving!

(*The little group pushes against the wall with all their might and slowly the wall begins to recede. As the wall is pushed back a dim, just perceptible light begins coming through the windows and with it the soft, muted sound of birds.*)

JACK: Keep pushing!

(*They push harder and as they push the stone recedes and the light becomes brighter and the sound of birds becomes louder. In the middle of the effort Terry's body begins to shudder. It is clear she is weeping.*)

EDDY: Can we rest a second, Dad? (*He gets Jack's attention and points at the weeping Terry.*)
JACK: What's wrong, Terry, you're pale as a ghost.
TERRY: Daddy, Eddy, I can't go with you.
JACK: We're not going anywhere, hon.
TERRY: Yes, you are and I can't go with you there . . . ever.
JACK: Where do you mean?
TERRY: You'll find out. (*She struggles to hold back her tears.*)
EDDY: What is it, Terry?

TERRY: I've got to go back now, I hear Elly calling. (*She backs away.*) There are some places that will never meet. I guess that's because all of us are part Thing. And someday, some of us will never meet again. (*She continues backing towards her wall.*) In a strange way it makes us all one like blind creatures filling an endless well getting wetter and wetter and blacker and blacker, with my tongue in your mouth and your feet in my stomach. Someday I may never *ever* see you again but just right now and now and now. (*She has backed up to her wall. The panel slides open and a strange red glow fills the room. There is the sound of pulsating steam and the humming of machinery. She stands pausing at the threshold. Then suddenly she runs to Eddy and Jack and throws her arms around them. Then suddenly she dashes away from them into the opening in her wall, calling as she runs.*) Goodbye, I remember . . .

(*Eddy runs to Terry's wall but it is closed tight.*)

EDDY: Terry! Terry! Dad, what happened? What was she talking about?
JACK: I don't know. We won't need her for this thing.
EDDY: Dad, don't be so cold.
JACK: Don't get melodramatic. Come on, let's push thing this out.

(*Eddy joins Jack and again they begin pushing against the stone.*)

EDDY: (*Grunting.*) It won't budge.
JACK: Come on, put some belly into it.

(*Again they dig into the work, pushing with all their strength. Again the huge block begins to recede and as it does the light continues to grow and the sounds of the birds becomes louder.*)

EDDY: Dad, it's really moving!
JACK: Yes, I know, keep pushing!

(*As they push the sound of the stone's grating becomes audible and the dawn breaks more and more until it fills the whole house with light.*)

JACK: (*Grunting as he exerts himself.*) Come on just a bit more!

(*They heave and shove and as they do the stone moves and the dawn breaks more and more. Jack and Eddy stop.*)

JACK: Are you ready?
EDDY: (*Out of breath and excited.*) Yes!
JACK: Okay then . . .

(*They shove and suddenly the huge stone falls away and light blazes through the hole. Out on the backdrop there is the color of a primeval dawn and mountains. There are birds singing joyously everywhere and soft breezes. Eddy and Jack stick their heads out the hole in the wall.*)

EDDY: God, look Dad!
JACK: Yes, I can see!

(*Jill suddenly appears on the other side of the hole. She is beautiful with her hair piled up on her head and wearing a Grecian robe. She is carrying an empty bird cage with the cage door open.*)

JILL: Well, what are you two waiting for? Come on out. Tammy's here too.
TAMMY: (*She too is on the other side, radiantly attired.*) Come on out, you guys, I'm playing Hippolytus.
JILL: But you've got to leave everything behind.

(*Jack and Eddy strip.*)

JACK: (*Now naked, steps through.*) Like the skin of the snake.
EDDY: (*Also naked, and stepping through.*) I think I remember this place.
JILL: Here, clean up after yourselves.

(*They pick up the stone and replug the hole. The stone is now very light. They, of course, disappear behind the wall. Upstairs there is a ringing of an alarm clock. Then another one joins it. And then another one. And then from another room the sound of a clock. Then one after another, each alarm clock is turned off. Jill comes out of the master bedroom in a bathrobe singing to herself. She stops on the landing.*)

JILL: Now don't turn those alarms off prematurely, that is *before* you're out of bed. (*She comes down the steps.*) I love it. Children all around me. My husband. A growing nation full of schools. (*She goes to the table and begins setting it.*) And now, at last, it's breakfast.

(*Eddy begins singing scales in his room. Then from Tammy's room comes the sound of an electric razor.*)

JILL: (*Shouting up at the rooms as she continues to set the table.*) Jack, remember not to use the electric razor with shaving lather.
EDDY: (*Sticking his head out the door, his face covered with lather.*) It's not Dad, it's Tammy.
JILL: Tammy, remember the last time you used the electric on your arm pits, it gave you a rash.
EDDY: (*Snickering.*) She's not using it on her pits, she's shaving her wig.
JILL: Tammy, don't use the electric on your wig, the plastic gets caught in the gears. And Eddy, don't be such a snitch.

(*Eddy sticks his head back in his room and closes his door.*)

JILL: (*Calling as she sets the table.*) Jack, are you up yet?
JACK: (*His voice muffled behind the door.*) Yes, honey.
JILL: Jack, is anything wrong? You be careful now, we don't want any mishaps.

(*Jack opens his door. His head is stuffed up into a white porcelain pitcher.*)

JILL: (*Seeing Jack's state.*) Eddy?
EDDY: (*The top of his head also covered with lather as well as his entire face.*) Yes, Mom?
JILL: Help your father.
EDDY: Jesus Christ, Dad! What happened to your face?
JACK: I was trying to rinse out my eyes.
EDDY: Yuk-yuk. Here, let's go to the bathroom.

(*They go into the master bedroom.*)

JILL: Tammy? Tammy?
TAMMY: (*From within her room.*) Yes, Mother, I'm awake.
JILL: This family is awake! Come on, it's breakfast!

(*Everyone comes out from upstairs and stands on the landing looking down at Jill. Eddy is in a nice black suit, Tammy wears a green dress and Jack is in an overcoat and bowler.*

They softly applaud Jill.)

EDDY: (*After they have finished clapping.*) Mom. (*He smiles warmly and tenderly at Jill.*) Thank you.
TAMMY: (*Stepping forward.*) Thank you, Mother.
JACK: Honey, the Visigoths kept it warm between the loins of horses.
JILL: And?
JACK: And what's for breakfast?
JILL: Me.

(*She takes her shoes off, steps up onto the table and lies down on it. There is a knocking on the front door.*)

EDDY: Don't get up Mom, I'll get it.

(*He dashes down the stairs and opens the door. Terry is standing there. The wind is blowing and she has an open umbrella and a cute little dress. She looks exactly like the 1941 Morton's Salt girl. In fact, she is carrying a box of salt.*)

TERRY: When it rains, it pours. (*She steps in, the salt pouring out in a trail behind her.*)

(*They all come and stand around the table where Jill is lying.*)

EDDY: Here Mom. (*He goes over and gets a blanket and throws it over Jill.*)
TAMMY: (*Seating herself.*) Oh aren't you gallant.
JACK: (*Seating himself.*) Mamacopia.

(*They pull various fruits from under the blanket.*)

JACK: Eddy, I heard what happened at school yesterday. And I want to tell you that you handled yourself well under the circumstances. But you shouldn't let a guy beat you up. No matter what. Even if it hurts you, you should keep swinging. Listen, if he knocks you down just get up and keep swinging. And then if he knocks you down just get up and keep swinging just like Jason and the Argonauts. Remember those skeletons that kept coming up out of the earth even though the hero sliced them to pieces? They just kept coming up and coming up, the little pieces would turn into skeletons and would just keep popping up from the ground as if his own violence had bred them. That's what you've got to do too. Down you go. Up you pop. Down you go. Up you pop. And up you pop and up you pop until he exhausts himself on you and icy fear will creep into his veins. It will! And he'll see that no matter how hard he hits you, you won't cry. Look at me, Eddy. Just make little sniffs like this when you want to cry.

See. Little sniffs and bury your eyes into your head like a dead man and get up off of the ground, bleeding and all and come at him with your arms rounded in the cosmic mudra and head at him like a missile towards his heart. Remember that he has a beating heart. It must beat and it must beat and it must beat. And it will pull you to it like a heat guided lover. So keep yourself towards that heat delivered up by his beating heart and sniff your tears back and if he round-houses you like this, and your head snaps to the side like this, let a flag of your blood whip out at him like a sun spurt and splash his face with it so that his heart quickens at the thought of it. When his face is hit by your blood it will worry his heart and it will beat faster and he will begin to strain from the ages of absolute non-existence from which his heart issued itself up like a dream. And Eddy, he will become afraid and his blood will chill and he will stop pushing you around, the dirty, ugly mother-fucker will stop pushing you around and when he sees you on the street he will smile at you kindly. He will be more understanding. You will have him in your HASPS! And there will be girls in your life like you've never known before. The age of heroes is eternal and anyone who tells you differently is merely trying to hold you down. Don't let them hold you down! When you are a hero then the age of heroes is! And they will say "Heroes live!" But where there are no heroes the age of heroes lies dormant like spring ground under snow. There are no signs to watch for. You are the sign. Will you do that for me? Don't go down!
EDDY: Yes, Dad. I won't go down.

(*Eddy gets up from the table.*)

EDDY: (*Bending over and kissing Jill.*) Thanks, Mom.

(*Jack gets up and accompanies Eddy to the door. He stops and looks at Eddy.*)

JACK: Goddamn it, Eddy, I hope I did right by you in your childhood.
EDDY: You did, Dad. (*He puts a hand on Jack's shoulder.*) Thanks.
JACK: (*Puts a hand on Eddy's shoulder.*) Ditto.
EDDY: (*Calling to Tammy.*) Sis?
TAMMY: (*Looking up from her fruit.*) Yes?
EDDY: (*Earnestly.*) Have a nice day.
TAMMY: You too, Eddy.
EDDY: Terry?
TERRY: Yes, Eddy, me too, I too will have a nice one.
JACK: Be cool, honey.
EDDY: (*Earnestly.*) I will.
JACK: (*Pointing at the door.*) Into it.
EDDY: Bang bang. (*He takes a deep breath, opens the door and dives out of sight.*)
JACK: (*Chuckling to himself, excited.*) Goddamn, goddamn! I can feel this day

coming up through my shoes. I'm going to make it this time. I'm going to beat him to work. I even think I know where he leaves it. (*He turns around and goes to the closet, opens the door and pulls out a brief case and holds it over his head.*) See? (*He laughs.*) See? (*Then he pauses.*) Only one thing. I have to go to the bathroom.

JILL: Don't do it, Jack. Go and do it in the sink if you have to but stay out of the upstairs bathroom.

JACK: (*Uneasy.*) You're right. I'm obsessing. No, no, into the sink or my pants. But honey, I've got to . . . (*He goes over and whispers into Jill's ear.*)

JILL: That's okay, we have a garbage disposal. Tammy, throw a sheet over your father.

TAMMY: With pleasure.

(*Jack sits on the sink and Tammy throws a sheet over him. Jack's pants drop from beneath the sheet.*)

JILL: Haven't you two buttoned up your little squabble?

TAMMY: I don't think we ever will, Mom.

JILL: (*Knowingly.*) Oh yes, you will, someday.

TAMMY: You know this is hopeless. He'll never go outside.

(*Suddenly Jack gives a holler and disappears into the sink leaving an empty sheet.*)

JILL: I don't know honey, somehow I keep hoping. But perhaps you're right. Perhaps the world is only Taughter.

TAMMY: Talkter?

JILL: Talkter.

TAMMY: What do you mean "Talkter?"

JILL: It's like "laughter" only it's talking. Well, pull this blanket off me. (*She gets up off the table.*) Terry, you haven't said a thing.

TERRY: That's because God didn't give me anything to say until just now.

TAMMY: I'm going, Mom.

JILL: See you tonight.

TAMMY: (*Stops by the door.*) Oh, Mom?

JILL: Yes?

TAMMY: I had the most wonderful night last night.

JILL: You did?

TAMMY: Yes, it was sort of a breakthrough. I had a lot of dreams . . . (*Her voice trails off and she looks at Jill.*) You were in them. (*She looks at Terry.*) So were you.

JILL: And so was I.

TERRY: Me too.

(*They all laugh.*)

TAMMY: You know what I'm going to be when I grow up?
JILL AND TERRY: What?
TAMMY: I'm going to be a personal psychologist.
JILL: (*Going to the closet and pulling out a huge hat with an enormous green feather.*) Here, try this on for size.
TAMMY: (*Putting on the hat.*) Oh, I feel just like Dorothy and the Tornado!
JILL: Watch out for the winds of time.

(*Tammy steps out the door and is whisked away by a powerful wind.*)

JILL: (*Turning to Terry.*) Now, my little gear cutter, it's time for you to vacillate.
TERRY: (*Laughing.*) If you only knew. Well, (*she heads for the wall*) I'd best be in. (*She stops and turns towards Jill.*) Mom, this afternoon is going to be very sunny and warm. Preschoolers are going to be riding their trikes and the sidewalks are going to be all white with long strips of sunshine and the grass will be amazingly green. Open all of the windows and go upstairs and make love. "Today." (*Said like "goodbye."*)
JILL: Today.

(*The panel in the wall slides open. There is an alien sound of throbbing, humming engines. It is as if there was an enormous place down there. Terry waves sweetly and the door slides shut in front of her.*)

(*Jill opens all of the windows. The light streams in. The sound of a clear spring day is heard. Preschoolers are playing outside and there is the sound of birds and distant laughter. Jill is humming. She looks up toward the master bedroom. She lets her bathrobe fall from her. She is naked.*)

JILL: (*Calling sweet and low.*) Jack?

(*She climbs the stairs as the lights fade into darkness.*)

END

Playwrights' Biographies

Rochelle Owens has written more than a dozen plays since 1965. They include the award-winning *Futz, Istanboul, Beclch, Kontraption,* and *The Karl Marx Play.* Her plays have appeared in the U.S. and abroad. *Chucky's Hunch,* which opened in 1981 at Theatre for the New City in New York earned an Obie for its solo character. Two volumes of Owens's plays have been published: *Futz and What Came After* and *The Karl Marx Play and Others.* She has also published several volumes of her poetry.

Wallace Shawn is a playwright and actor. Besides his *A Thought in Three Parts,* Shawn has written the Obie-winner *Our Late Night* (directed by Andre Gregory), *Marie and Bruce,* and an adaptation of *The Mandrake,* all produced at the Public Theater. Shawn has appeared in several theatre productions, in the films *Annie Hall* and *Atlantic City,* and the highly acclaimed *My Dinner With Andre,* which he also wrote.

Len Jenkin has seen his plays produced in several U.S. theatres. An adaptation of *Candide* was presented at the Guthrie Theatre. Other plays include *Gogol, New Jerusalem, The Death and Life of Jesse James* and, most recently, *Dark Ride.* He has also written for television and film.

Harry Kondoleon had his first production, *Rococo,* at the Yale Repertory Winterfest in 1981. Several of his plays have been produced since then: *The Brides, Self Torture and Strenuous Exercise, Fairy Garden* and *The Cote D'Azur Triangle.* His teleplay, *Clara Toil,* was part of the 1982 Eugene O'Neill National Playwrights Conference. His latest play, *Christmas on Mars,* is to be produced by Playwrights Horizons in New York.

John O'Keefe is a California playwright and performer. Many of his plays have been seen at the Magic Theatre in San Francisco since 1973: *Chamber Piece, Jimmy Beam, The Saints of Fr. Lyons, Ghosts,* and *All Night Long.* He is a founding member of one of the Bay Area's important theatre groups, the Blake Street Hawkeyes. O'Keefe's *Bercilak's Dream* was produced at the Bay Area Playwrights Festival in the summer of 1982.